Daniel W Perkins

Practical Common Sense Guide Book

Through the World's Industrial and Cotton Centennial Exposition....

Daniel W Perkins

Practical Common Sense Guide Book
Through the World's Industrial and Cotton Centennial Exposition....

ISBN/EAN: 9783337203351

Printed in Europe, USA, Canada, Australia, Japan

Cover: Foto ©ninafisch / pixelio.de

More available books at **www.hansebooks.com**

PRACTICAL COMMON SENSE

GUIDE BOOK

THROUGH

—THE WORLD'S—
INDUSTRIAL AND COTTON CENTENNIAL
EXPOSITION

AT

NEW ORLEANS.

GIVING IN BRIEF FORM THE BEST THINGS TO BE SEEN IN EACH DEPARTMENT, AND JUST HOW AND WHERE TO SEE THEM.

Also, the Principal Places of Interest in and about the City.

NOT ONLY MAKING ONE CERTAIN OF SEEING THE BEST THINGS, BUT MAKING AN IMMENSE SAVING OF TIME.

HARRISBURG, PA.:
LANE S. HART, PRINTER AND BINDER.
1885.

U. S. BUILDING INDEX.

	Page.		Page.
Alabama,	27	Missouri,	27
Arkansas,	27	Maryland,	29
Arizona,	16	Miscellaneous,	74
Agricultural Department,	36	Nebraska,	9
California,	17	New Mexico,	13
Center, or General Government,	32	Nevada,	17
Colorado,	15	New Hampshire,	22
Connecticut,	21	New Jersey,	30
Colored People's Department,	44	New York,	30
Dakota,	9	North Carolina,	31
Delaware,	29	Navy Department,	38
East Tenn. and Va. R. R.,	13	Oregon,	12
Engraving and Printing Bureau,	37	Ohio,	21
Electric Railway,		Places of Interest in and About New Orleans,	3
Educational Department,	40		
Florida,	32	Pennsylvania,	29
Foote, A., Mineral Collection,	28	Patent Office,	35
Gallery,	72	Post-office,	
General Directions for use of Guide,	6	Queen and Crescent R. R.,	28
Georgia,	28	Richmond and Danville R. R. System,	13
Geology and Ethnology,	33		
Greely Relief,	38	Rhode Island,	23
Iowa,	7	South Carolina,	32
Idaho,	11	Smithsonian Institute,	33
Illinois,	18	State Department,	38
Indiana,	19	Texas,	23
Kansas,	10	Tennessee,	26
Kentucky,	26	U. S. Building,	7
Louisiana,	24	U. S. R. R. Commission,	34
Land Office,	34	Vermont,	21
Light-House and Coast Survey,	37	Virginia,	31
Minnesota,	8	Wyoming Territory,	12
Montana Territory,	12	Wisconsin,	18
Michigan,	19	West Virginia,	30
Massachusetts,	22	War Department,	37
Maine,	23	Women's Department,	39
Mississippi,	26	Washington Territory,	11

MAIN BUILDING INDEX.

A.

	Page.
American Machinery Co.,	62
Am. Paper Box Co.,	47
Atkins, E. C., & Co.,	62
Am. Standard Drop Shot Co.,	47
Am. Machine Co.,	48
Ala. and Ga. Manufacturing Co.,	51
Andrew Bros.,	50
Appleton, D.,	52
American Wine Co.,	52
American Well Works,	56
Avery, B. F., & Sons,	56
Automatic Ice-Cream Freezer,	—
Allen, S. L., & Co.,	56
Anderson's Fruit Butters, &c.,	54
Allen Car-Wheel Co.,	60
Allison Manufacturing Co.,	57
Aikman, James, & Co.,	61
Armstrong, F., & Co.,	61
Altman, Taylor Thresher,	61
Atlantic Eng. Co.,	62
Austin, Opdyke & Co.,	62
American Ship Windlass Co.,	—
American Ultra Marine Works,	48
Alaska Down Co.,	49
American Hosiery Co.,	51
American Hair Brush Co.,	52
Allen & Gaiter,	53
Anheuser-Busch Brewers,	53
Arm and Hammer Brand Soda,	53
American Live Stock Salt Roller Co.,	55
American Salt Co.,	56
American Scale Co.,	57
American Steam Gauge Co.,	60
Ames Iron Works,	60
Alling's Lightning Dish Washer,	60
American Wire Nail Co.,	61
American Diamond Rock Boring Co.,	64
American Hoop Dresser,	64

	Page.
Allen, E. P.,	64
American Pin Co.,	65
Anderson, C. E., (gal.,)	78
Abbott Buggy Co., (gal.,)	77
Abbott, A. O., (gal.,)	77
Austria,	—
Atkins, G. F.,	75
American Soap Stone Co.,	75
Albro, E. D., & Co.,	75

B.

Burhard, George, & Sons,	—
Bean, T. A., & L. L.,	—
Blades, Carlton,	52
Blatz, V.,	—
Brooklyn Shirt Co.,	51
Baker, Walter & Co.,	52
Bailey, J. T., & Co.,	50
Burroughs & Montford,	49
Barbour's Flax Thread,	49
Bridgeford & Co.,	48
Buck's Stove and Range Co.,	48
Bowers, W. C.,	48
Baltimore Sun Office,	48
Black Diamond File Co.,	48
Bent, Samuel, & Co.,	48
Biliousine Patent Medicine,	47
Bonstein's Patent Pin Hook,	50
Brown, B. F.,	50
Burt, Edwin, & Co.,	50
Belding Bros., & Co.,	50
Bullard Repeating Arms Co.,	50
Beck, Joseph, & Co.,	50
Bakewell & Mullins,	50
Benheim, August, & Bauer,	50
Bergner & Engel,	52
Buckeye Harvesting Machine,	56
Birdsall Mfg. Co.,	56
Brown Mfg. Co.,	55
Boyd, W. L., & Bros.,	
Blount's True-Blue Plows,	54

PRACTICAL COMMON SENSE GUIDE BOOK.

	Page.		Page.
Barnard, G. D., & Co.,	54	Beck, Fred'k., (gal.,)	78
Boker's Stomach Bitters,	53	Buford's, J. H., Sons, (gal.,)	78
Bickford, G. M.,	60	Brunacci, R. E.,	67
Bailey Wringing Machine,	60	Boncinelli, Gioni,	67
Boston Woven Hose Co.,	60	Berg & Co.,	76
Baltimore Car Wheel Co.,	60	Becker Bros.,	74
Brown, W. H. Sons,	59	Belgium,	59
Burkhart, True & Co.,		British Honduras,	72
Besse, Dr. H.,		Brazil,	73
Blaymyer, J. S.,			
Bliss, E. W.,	63	**C.**	
Blackmer & Post,	61	Cabott, Samuel, Jr.,	47
Boston Belting Co.,	61	Cassidy & Miller,	50
Bergner & Co.,	61	Cahill's Alma Shoe Polish,	50
Baltimore Bell and Brass Works,	61	Cheesborough Manufacturing Co.,	49
Beaudry & Cunningham,	62	Cibil's Beef Extract Co.,	49
Buffalo Forge Co.,	62	Charter Oak Stove Co.,	48
Buffalo Scale Co.,	57	Colt's Fire Arms Co.,	48
Bowers, T. H., & Co.,	62	Colgate & Co.,	48
Brown, Fred'k.,	47	Chief of Transportation, office,	47
Bromley, J., & Sons,	49	Chief of Installation, office,	48
Bollmann, E. & M.,	52	Cross, F. O.,	48
Best, Philip,	52	Corticelli Spool Silk,	50
Bamer Packing Co.,	52	Coffin, Altemus & Co.,	50
Bridgeport Wood Finishing Co.,	53	Chalmette Mills Fertilizers,	50
Berkley & Co.,	53	Clark's O. N. T. Spool Cotton,	51
Baldwin, E. J.,	53	Chamberlin Cartridge Co.,	51
Bruce's, George, Son & Co.,	54	Canfield Dress Shield Co.,	51
Baldwin Dry Air Refrigerator,	55	Chase, A. B.,	51
Boyer. W. L., & Bro.,	55	Colborn, A., & Co.,	52
Brown's Corn Planter Works,	55	Cambria Iron Co.,	56
Bradley, David, & Co.,	56	Cincinnati Water Elevator Co.,	56
Blymer Mfg. Co.,	57	Champion Iron Fence Co.,	57
Barrett, J.,	60	Cornish, Curtis & Greene,	56
Burkey Foundry Co.,	60	Carter, E. D.,	55
Brown Cotton Gin Co.,	63	Cox & Poynter,	54
Barbour's Cotton Gin,	63	California Chocolate Co.,	53
Benjamin & Fischer,	64	Crane Bros.,	53
Beach, H. L.,	64	Carlisle Mfg. Co.,	59
Bridesburg Mfg. Co.,	65	Cold Storage Rooms,	59
Brownel, G. & L.,	65	Chapman Valve Mfg. Co.,	61
Brunswick, Balke, Collender & Co.,		Cincinnati Corrugating Co.,	61
(gal.,)	76	Coleman, H. D.,	61
Berry Bros., (gal.,)	77	Cooper, Hewit & Co.,	63
Baker, Sloo & Co., (gal.,)	77	Chattanooga Foundry Pipe Co.,	61
Buermann, A., (gal.,)	78	Cooper, Jones & Co.,	61
Boardman, F., (gal.,)	78	Coleman's Shaft, &c.,	61
Buddington Dress-Cutting Machine,		Chaffee, S., & Burdenberg,	61
(gal.,)	78	Cincinnati Brass Co.,	61

	Page.		Page.
Cleveland & Hardinwick,	62	Dietz Manufacturing Co.,	
Coes, C. W.,	62	Dairy Exhibit of Wisconsin,	
Cincinnati Barbed Wire Co.,	63	Dolph, A. M., & Co.,	60
Cincinnati Safe Co.,	49	Degraw, Aymer & Co.,	59
Clark, Herbert & Co.,	49	Diamond Emery Wheel Co.,	63
Clark's Mile End Spool Cotton,	65	Dodge Manufacturing Co.,	56-63
Clawson, H., & Son,	53	Ditson, H., & Sons,	61
Continental Brewing Co.,	53	Delamater, C. H., & Co.,	62
Cavarro Wine Co.,	53	Demuth, Wm., & Co.,	53
Croft & Allen,	53	Durham Tobacco Works,	52
Carson & Brown,	54	Donnell, J. F., & Co.,	52
Cleveland Carriage Co.,	55	Dozier & Weyl,	52
Canedy, W. E.,	55	Dwight Mf'g Co.,	52
Chess-Carley Co.,	55	Dennison Mf'g Co.,	54
Chamberlain Plow Co,	57	Deere, Mansur & Co.,	54
Combination Gas Machine Co.,	60	Dejan & Carter,	55
Clark Gas Engine Co.,		Dunn Edge Tool Co.,	
Coes, C. W.,		Davis' Fire-escape,	56
Colwell Iron Works,	64	Dietz Fruit Evaporator,	57
Coble, M.,		Detroit Blower Co.,	60
Curtis, James F.,	64	Dietz, R. E.,	60
Coats, J. & P.,	64	Dowdell, A. W.,	65
Cooper & McKee, (gal.,)	78	Dennel, R., & Bro., (gal.,)	77
Crane Bros., (gal.,)	77	Dexter Spring Co., (gal.,)	77
Christina Carriage Factory, (gal.,)	77	Demerest, A. T., & Co., (gal.,)	77
Columbus Buggy Co., (gal.,)	77	Davis, H. W., & Co., (gal.,)	77
Cunningham, James, Son & Co., (gal.,)	77	Daisy Sewing Machine Co., (gal.,)	78
Chong, Haing,	66	Duffy, L. J., (gal.,)	78
Canini, J. F.,	67	Dape Bros. & Kugemann, (gal.,)	78
Conley, C. J., & Co.,	76	Dodany, H. M.,	67
Clagui, Schlicht & Field,	76	Decanville's Portable Railway,	68
Caw's Ink,	75	Delpit, Tobacco and Snuff,	75
Colby & Co.,	75	Duryea's Mazena,	75
Columbian Type Writer,	76	**E.**	
Christian, Thomas,	75	Electrine Magic Cleaner,	47
Collier White Lead Co.,	74	Egyptian Chemical Co.,	47
China,	71	Engelbach, T.,	47
		Excelsior Pottery Works,	47
D.		Elizabeth Paraffine Co.,	47
Denler's Butters,	47	Empire Pottery Works,	49
Detroit Safe Co.,	63	Evans, John,	47
Director General's Office,	47	Erkenbrecker, A.,	52
Detroit, Michigan, Stove Works,	48	Empire Lamp Co,	51
Danziger, D.,	51	Eavenson, J., & Sons,	53
Denny, Poor & Co.,	50	E. India Fancy Goods,	53
Doherty & Wadsworth,	50	Eastwood, Benj.,	60
Durrie & McCarty,	47	Eberhard Mf'g Co.,	61
Dunlap & Co.,	51	Eclipse Blacking Brush,	62

	Page.
Engle Cotton Gin Co.,	57
Enterprise Mf'g Co.,	63
Erie Preserving Co.,	52
Elgin Watch Co.,	53
Edison Light Co.,	53
Esterbrook Pen Co.,	54
Emerson, Talcott & Co.,	55
Exhaust Ventilator Co.,	60
Excelsior Steam Pump,	60
Egan Wood-Working Machinery,	64
Edgefield and Nashville Manuf'g Co., (gal.,)	78
Elkhart Mfg. Co., (gal.,)	77
Excelsior Top Co., (gal.,)	77
Errico, F.,	67
Eastern Mfg. Co.,	—
England,	69

F.

	Page.
Finlay, G. R., & Co.,	48
Favorite Stove Works,	48
Fong, T.,	48
Freman's Face Powder,	48
Fisher, J. W.,	48
Fields, Wm., & Co.,	52
Fairbanks' Scales,	54
Frick & Co.,	56
Foos Mfg. Co.,	55
Fairchild Gold Pen Co.,	53
French Spring Co.,	59
Filter Tanks and Reservoirs,	—
Fairbank Canning Co.,	—
Fenton, Wm. B.,	63
Flanigan, P. J.,	62
Fay, J. A., & Co.,	63
Franklin Knitting Works,	49
Fletcher Mfg. Co.,	49
Farmers' Fertilizer Co.,	54
Freeport Machine Co.,	60
Fulton Iron Works,	63
Forsaith Machinery Co.,	64
Fenner, E. C., (gal.,)	77
Farr, Wm. M., (gal.,)	77
Fair Haven Slate Co., (gal.,)	78
Friedrich, W., (gal.,)	78
France,	68
Farfalla, Alla,	67
Fountain Ink Co.,	75

G.

	Page.
Gillam's Sons,	47
Granite Iron Co.,	47
Ganche's Sons,	49
Griffin, Smith & Co.,	48
Globe Pickle Co.,	52
Gray, A. W., & Sons,	55
Gardner Piano,	53
Grunewald Piano,	53
General Directions for Main Building,	46
General Description of Main Building,	45
Gents' Water-Closet,	61
Gandy Belting Co.,	61
Graphite Lubricating Co.,	61
Grovet, F. L.,	62
Gleason, E. & F.,	63
Goodell & Waters,	63
Goodyear Rubber Co.,	50
Globe Planter,	56
Graham, L., & Son,	60
Gibson, George,	64
Gordon's Planer,	64
Gilbert & Bennett Mfg. Co.,	64
Gast, August, & Co.,	65
Glass Engraver,	66
Ginoris, M. & J., (gal.,)	79
Gardner & Co., (gal.,)	76
Gunold, C., & Co., (gal.,)	78
Gillett & Gottschalk, (gal.,)	78
Globe Knitting Co., (gal.,)	78
Goldschmidt, M., & Son,	67
Griscuolo, Michele,	67
Garobolo & Co.,	67
Gross Pen Co.,	75
Gutta Percha Paint Co.,	75
Germany,	70
Guatemala,	72

H.

	Page.
Hall & Brown,	63
Hoyt, J. B., & Co.,	61
Hecht, Jewelry, &c,	49
Hance Bros. & White,	47
Hoffman, J. T.,	50
Hart, E. J., & Co.,	47
Heinemann, T. W.,	49
Halliday, G. V.,	

	Page.		Page.
Herbert, Clark & Co.,		Hertts Bros., (gal.,)	76
Hutchinson, Pierce & Co.,	49	Heywood Bros. & Co., (gal.,)	76
Hemingray Glass Co.,	48	Henderson Buggy Co., (gal.,)	77
Holmes & Coutts,	50	Heald & Jones, (gal.,)	77
He-No Tea Co.,	50	Hall Mfg. Co., (gal.,)	77
Holmes, D H., & Co.,	51	Hubbard Hammock Co., (gal.,)	79
Hart, Junius,	51	Hart, E. J., & Co.,	76
Haraszthy & Co.,	52	Hemsheim, S.,	75
Hughes, M. T.,	57	Hengley & Challenge, Roller Skates,	75
Hall, J. H., & Co.,	56		
Hutchins Refrigerating Car,	56	**I.**	
Herbner & Sons,	55	International Pottery Co.,	49
Holt, Hiram, & Co.,	55	Iowa Farming Tool Co.,	48
Hastings Gold Leaf,	54	Inman Steamship Line,	48
Heinz Bros.,	53	Iveys' Adjustable Box, &c ,	55
Hancock Inspirator Co.,	60	Iron Barbed Wire Co.,	63
Humane Society,	—	Ideal Coffee Pot Mfg. Co.,	47
Hard Rubber Co.,	47	Ivers & Pond,	53
Horstman Bros.,	49	Israel, F.,	64
Hough & Ford,	49	Italy,	67
Hughes, R. P., & Co.,	50	Indianapolis Terra Cotta Co.,	75
Helms' Snuff,	53		
Holman, A. J., & Co.,	52	**J.**	
Hartel, T. T.,	53	Johnston's Fluid Beef,	50
Hill Bros.,	53	Jennings, A. G., & Son,	50
Harper Bros ,	53	Jarvis Brandy Co.,	52
Hahn, A., & Co.,	53	Jackson, R. W.,	58
Halls, Evan,	53	Jackson, Junius,	61
Hallihan, John,	53	Johns, Thos.,	61
Hyatt, A. W.,	54	Johns, H. W.,	61
Holyoke Paper Co.,		Jackson & Tyler,	62
Henning Bros.,	55	Jillson & Palmer,	63
Hartshorn Spring Bed,	55	Jenney Electric Light Co.,	53
Haven & Co.,	55	Johnson & Field,	55
Hercules Mfg. Co.,	55	Johnson, A. M.,	57
Homestead Fertilizer,	55	Jones, Phineas, & Co., (gal.,)	77
Harron & Dexter,	56	Japan,	71
Higgins Eureka Dairy Salt,	56	Jamaica,	70
Harrison Machine Works,	57		
Holmes & Co.,	57	**K.**	
Hanson, A.,	60	Keystone Watchcase Co.,	76
Huyett & Smith,	60	Keller, J. H.,—O. J. Keller in	
Howe Scale Co.,	57	charge,	49
Hoe, R., & Co ,	60	King, John,	47
Hotchkiss Boiler Cleaner,	61	King's Food,	52
Holmes, E. B.,	64	Kranch & Bach,	51
Harden's Grenade Fire Extinguisher,	64	Kalbfleish, Martin & Sons,	52
		Kingsland & Ferguson,	
Hopedale Machine Co.,	65	Kemp & Burpee Manufacturing Co.,	55,56

	Page.		Page.
Kruse, Check & Adding Machine,	54	**M.**	
Kanny, A. B.,	54	Mast & Co.,	56
Krell, Albert,	53	Myers, A. & H.,	47
Knoxville Car Wheel Co.,	59	McBryers, W. H.,	47
Keonig & Bauer,	60	Manning Co.,	48
Kalamazoo R. R. Velocipede Co.,	63	Mich. Stove Co.,	48
Kilpstein, A.,	47	Miller, William, & Co.,	48
Kendall's Manufacturing Co.,	49	McKinnon, C.,	48
Kirk, J., & Co.,	53	Monumental Bronze Co.,	48
Kirk's Perfumery,	53	Metallic Burial Co.,	49
Keummerle Vegetable, Ivory Goods, &c.,	65	Mississippi Mills,	49
		Mott, C. E.,	49
Klein, Mathias, (gal.,)	77	Marshall, J. T.,	50
Kentucky Furniture Co., (gal.,)	76	Myers, Fred. J., Mfg. Co.,	50
Koons, G., (gal.,)	78	Mayers, H. J.,	51
Kaemper, M., (gal.,)	78	Meriden Britannia Co.,	50
Kursherdt & Co., (gal.,)	78	Mahr's Sons, H.,	52
Kaffel & Freres,	68	Mitchell & Co.,	52
		Mason & Hamlin Organs, &c.,	52
L.		Michaelobitz, Ernie,	—
Lalance & Grosjean Manufacturing Co.,	47	Moline Plow Co.,	57
		Maitre, R.,	56
Lyon, Amassa,	49	Michigan Scales Co.,	56
Lyons, I. L., & Co.,	48	Marvel & Williams,	56
Lehman, Abraham, & Co.,	49	Meikel, Thomas, & Co.,	56
Lucas, John, & Co.,	50	McCormick's Reapers,	56
Lancaster Mills,	52	Mann, William,	54
Lee's Patent Undergarments,	51	McAllister, H.,	54
Lundy, Smith & Co.,	59	Marks, A. A.,	54
Leviathan Belting Co.,	61	Meyer, J. H.,	54
Leffel, J., & Co.,	61	McMann & Bros.,	60
Laclede Fire Brick Co.,	62	Medart Patent Pulley Co.,	61
Leigh, F. A.,	63	Mason, A. W., & Co.,	61
Ladies' Dressing-room,	47	Moffett, A. W.,	63
Lebess, D. N., & Co.,	48	Maine Belting Co.,	61
LeGraf's Manufacturing Co.,	49	Mixter Saw Tools,	62
Luby, Dr. J.,	54	Moreley Bros.,	62
Lamar Cotton Cultivator,	54	Morse, F. H.,	62
Ladies' Toilet,	59	Marietta Hollow-Ware Co.,	47
Landon, Albert,	57	Mosler, Bahmann & Co.,	49
Lowrie, H. C.,	60	Marsok & Schottler,	50
Lufkin, E. T.,	62	Moir, John, & Son,	52
Leedon, T. L., & Co., (gal.,)	79	Moillard, Henry,	52
Lengert, G., & Son, (gal.,)	77	Maginnis Cotton Oil Works,	52
Little & Larkin, (gal.,)	77	Morris' Tobacco Works,	52
Labriola, M.,	67	Magnolia Ham Co.,	53
Lacroix, L.,	68	Murry Iron Works,	56
Luez, A.,	68	Mich. Axe and Tool Co.,	62
LePaige's Liquid Glue,	75	Myers, Osborn & Co.,	62

PRACTICAL COMMON SENSE GUIDE BOOK.

	Page.
Morse Cotton Compress,	64
Mitchell, Henry,	65
Mussey, J., & Co.,	65
Mathews, John,	66
Moore, J., & Co., (gal.,)	79
Matthews, Willard Co., (gal.,)	79
McCaw, Stephenson & Co., (gal.,)	78
McBride & Co., (gal.,)	78
Myers, H. J., (gal.,)	78
Mitchell, Robt., Furniture Co., (gal.,)	76
McIntosh Battery Co., (gal.,)	76
Marks Adj. Folding Chair Co., (gal.,)	77
Milburn Manufacturing Co., (gal.,)	77
Miller, D. G., (gal.,)	77
Monarch Rim Button Co., (gal.,)	77
Moser, Ludwig,	
Mari, Antonio,	67
McKeller, Smiths & Jordan,	76
Massman, J. & Co.,	75
Moseley & Co.,	76
Marderis Standard Scales,	74
Matthews, John,	74
Merchant & Co.,	74
Mexico,	73

N.

Norton Door Check and Spring,	47
Norfolk and New Brunswick Hosiery Co.,	49
Newark Machine Co.,	56
Nichols, Shepherd & Co.,	54
Nash & Bro.,	55
Novelty Iron Works,	63
National Sheet Metal Roofing Co.,	61, 62
New York Belting Co.,	61
Narraganset Machine Co.,	62
Nordyke, Harmon & Co.,	63
Northfield Knife Co.,	49
Noye, J. T., Manufacturing Co.,	55
New York Ramie Fibre Co.,	64
National Tube Works Co.,	65
Noyes, J. T.,	64
Nashville Trunk Manufy, (gal.,)	78
Nagl, Ralmond,	67
Neiter & Prestat,	68
New York Enamel Paint Co.,	75

O.

Ott & Brewer,	49
Over, Ewald,	55

	Page.
Otis & Gorsline,	62
Owensboro' Wheel Co.,	56
Ortmayer, A., & Son., (gal.,)	77
Olwatte Bros., (gal.,)	79
Olweri, Achile,	67
Olwoti Bros.,	67
Osgood's Scale Co.,	57

P.

Phœnix Glass Co.,	48
Powers & Wightman,	48
Parker Gun,	49
Penfield, E. C., & Co.,	51
Pond's Extract,	48
Pomenah Mills,	51
Pittsburgh Arms Co.,	51
Packard Organ Co.,	51
Porter's Evaporator,	
Pitts Threshing Machine,	56
Produce Exchange.	55
Perkins, P. C., & Co.,	55
Piano Mfg. Co.,	55
Palmer, E. C., & Co.,	54, 60
Pullman Car Co.,	57
Plumley & Ritchie,	63
Paige Mfg. Co.,	61
Penilliat, C.,	61
Pomeroy, A. H.,	63
Powell Tool Co.,	62
Pratt & Whitney Mfg. Co.,	62
Parker & Drigs,	47
Purdy & Nichols,	52
Pacific Mills,	53
Palmer, Charles T.,	56
Porter, J. F.,	57
Prouty Printing Press,	60
Payne, B. W., & Sons,	60
Pratt, Daniel,	63
Pease, C. G.,	64
Puffer, A. D., & Son,	64
Pioneer Silk Co.,	65
Phœnix Silk Mfg. Co.,	66
Palmer, Solon, (gal.,)	79
Potter, T., Sons & Co., (gal.,)	78
Palmenberg, J. R., (gal.,)	78
Peters & Calhon Co., (gal.,)	78
Phœnix Chair Co., (gal.,)	77
Plimpton, H. R., & Co., (gal.,)	77
Poulson & Egan, (gal.,)	76

	Page.		Page.
Petoreto, Grazlotie,	67	Russia,	58
Pouvier, R.,	68	Republic of Honduras,	70
Portevent & Favre,	75		
Pyle's Pearline,	75	**S.**	
Penn Wire Works,	75	Speer & Sons,	55
		Springfield Machine Co.,	57
Q.		Stong, J. E.,	57
Quint, S. H., & Son,	60	Sidney Steel Scraper Co.,	
Quinby, J. M., & Co., (gal.,)	77	Syracuse Chilled Plow Co.,	57
		Schwab, John,	52
R.		Southern Express Co.,	47
Reed's Tonic,	53	St. Louis Wrought Iron Range Co.,	48
Rotary Nutmeg Mill,	62	Stanley Works,	48
Reed & Co.,	47	Stearns, Fred., & Co.,	48
R. R. Ticket Office,	47	Seabury & Johnson,	49
Randolph Paper Box Co.,	49	Stein Mf'g Co.,	49
Roggers, Peet & Co.,	50	Simpson, Wm., Sons & Co.,	49
Remington Mfg. Co.,	50	Selz, Schwab & Co.,	49
Refrigerator,	59	Stribley & Co.,	50
Ross, E. W., & Co.,	55	Schlicter Jute Cordage Co.,	50
Remington Agrl. Works,	64	Superintendent of Agriculture,	54
Reed, D. C. & H. C., & Co.,	55	Sibley, G.,	54
Renton Bros.,	52	Schmidt & Zeigler,	53
Refrigerator,	56	Simons, W. L., & Bros.,	53
Roebling's, J. A., Sons,	63	Sutton, H. D., & Co.,	
Russell & Co.,	62	Smith, J. T.,	59
Rommarius, F.,	62	Stillwell & Bierce,	60
Robinson, E. A.,	52	Schwarzwaelder, A.,	57
Randolph, J. W., & English,	54	Scoville Manufacturing Co.,	62
Rushton, J. H.,	54	Sugar Apparatus,	62
Romkey, F. C.,	55	Sunny Side Tobacco Co.,	53
Roggers & Maher,	55	Schmidt, C. A.,	63
Riggs, A., & Bros.,	55	Strange, William, & Co.,	63
Rayner's Pressure Filter,	60	Standard Lighting Co.,	61
Reading Iron Co.,	60	Schroeder, Charles A., & Co.,	61
Remington Ag'l Co.,	54	Skinner & Wood,	61
Rutledge, S. C.,	64	Stephens, A. W., & Son,	61
Reading Bolt and Nutt Works,	64	Smith, W. J.,	62
Rose, Downs & Thompson,	64	Simonds' Manufacturing Co.,	62
Ready Cash Carrier, (gal.,)	78	Scarfe, B. F., & Sons,	62
Richmond Transfer Co., (gal.,)	77	Schwartz, Louis,	62
Randall, R. P., (gal.,)	77	Smith, G. T.,	63
Robinson & Hilt, (gal.,)	77	Starr, B. F., & Co.,	63
Reichle Bros., (gal.,)	77	Smith, Anthony, & Co.,	47
Renick, Curtis & Co., (gal.,)	77	Swift Manufacturing Co.,	49
Rumine, F.,		Sternberger, L. & S.,	49
Redden, A. L.,	76	Shriver & Co.,	50
Reichle Bros.,	74	Steel & Nissen,	50
Russell & Irwin,	74	Schlitz's Beer,	52

PRACTICAL COMMON SENSE GUIDE BOOK.

	Page.
Shaw Stocking Co.,	53
Semones, J. C.,	54
St. Lawrence Manufacturing Co.,	55
Simpson, McEntire & Co.,	56
Sheboygan Co. Dairy Board Trade,	56
Sprout, S. C. & J. M.,	57
Stratton, H. D., & Co.,	60
Sturtevant, B. F.,	60
Smith, H. B.,	63
Smith & Myers,	63
Stoltz, Frederick,	64
Sullivan Diamond Prospecting Drill,	64
Schwartz L., (gal.,)	76
Squire, Sidney & Co., (gal.,)	76
Schwartz, Joseph, (gal.,)	77
Shuler, A. F., (gal.,)	77
Steinbach, Adj. Baby Carriages, (gal.,)	77
Sayers & Scoville, (gal.,)	77
Studebaker Bros., (gal.,)	77
Singer Machine Co., (gal.,)	78
Schmit Bros., (gal.,)	78
Suhr & Hauptmann, (gal.,)	78
Shutz, M., (gal.,)	78
Standard Saloon Fixture Co., (gal.,)	78
Saginaw Mfg. Co., (gal.,)	79
Scholl, C. J., (gal.,)	79
Storm, Ed., (gal.,)	77
Schreppel & Walch,	67
Scribner, C., & Sons,	75
Southern White Lead Co.,	75
Stephenson, L., & Co.,	74
St. Louis Lead and Oil Co.,	75
Siam,	70
San Salvador,	
Spain	
Superior Drill Co.,	56
Scheffelin, W. H., & Co.,	
Schwartz, A., & Sons,	50
Speer's Wines,	52
Stetson, J. B.,	51
Spaulding, D. S.,	
Stieff Piano Co.,	51

T.

	Page.
Todd, Albert,	48
Taylor's Premium Cologne,	49
Thompson's Glove-Fitting Corset,	49
Tomson, P. C.,	52

	Page.
Touck, Jacob,	54
Thomas Clock Co.,	54
Taylor Cottonseed Crusher, &c.,	57
Thompson-Lewis,	52, 63
Taylor Mfg. Co.,	61
Thompson & Houston,	63
Tennis Gang-flooring Machine,	63
Tieman, C., & Co.,	48
Tichenor Hand Presses,	56
Tichenor, J. G.,	57
Thorp, H. H., & Co.,	60
Tuft, S. W.,	64
Thome, M., (gal.,)	78
Tolman, J. P., & Co., (gal.,)	78
Tisch, Charles, (gal.,)	76
Tausig, Maurice,	67
Thomas, L. H.,	76
Tennessee Lumber Co.,	75
Twisted Wire-Box Strap Co.,	74

U.

	Page.
Union Pottery Works,	49
Underwood's Chemical Ink,	52
Urbana Wine Co.,	53
U. S. Mint,	65
Union Mfg. Co., (gal.,)	78
Union School Fixture Co., (gal.,)	78
Union Paper Bag Co.,	75

V.

	Page.
Valentine & Co.,	75
Variety Iron Works,	63
Vehicle Spring Co.,	54
Valentine Meat Juice Co.,	52
Vail Bros,	48
Vester, Ferdinand,	54
Valsecchi, M.,	67
Veit, S.,	67

W.

	Page.
Watson's Portable Forge,	61
Whitney, A., & Sons,	60
White, S. S.,	54
Whiting Paper Co.,	54
Wo Sun Quog,	53
Western Union Telegraph,	47
Weaver & Shaudein,	48
Wyeth, John, & Bros.,	49
Wilmerding, Hoget & Co.,	49
Wolf & Relsing,	52

	Page.		Page.
Werlein, Philip,	51	White, John,	64
Williams' Evaporator,		Washburn & Moen Mfg. Co.,	64
Williams' Tension Wheel Co.,	56	Whitin Cotton Machinery,	65
Wrenn, Whitehurst & Co.,	56	Willimantic Cotton Co.,	65
Whitman Agrl. Mfg. Co.,	56	Weikel & Smith Spice Co.,	66
Wickes Pat. Refrigerator,	56	Waterbury Button Co.,	66
Wilbur, H. O., & Son,	53	Williams Manufacturing Co.,(gal.,)	77
Wood, B. D., & Co.,	61	Wakefield Rattan Co., (gal.,)	76
Wing's Disc Fan,	62	Weedsport Hoopskirt Co., (gal.,)	78
Walker, E. N., & Co.,	62	Wilson, J., (gal.,)	79
Wolf, M.,	53	Weydig, Martin, (gal.,)	78
Waymuth, A. D., & Co.,	63	Walch, Francis,	67
Woods, S. A., & Co.,	63	Waltham Watch Co.,	76
Winchester Repeating Arms Co.,		Wolf, John,	75
Waterbury Watch Co,	54	Wood, G. H., & Co.,	75
Weston, Byron,	54	Woods, H., & Son & Co.,	75
Wade, H. D., & Co.,	54	Wetherill, G. D., & Co.,	75
Walker, R. J.,	55		
Warren Fire Escape Co.,	55	Y.	
Wisconsin's Dairymens Association,	56	Young & Zerbe,	51
Weston Wheel Scraper Co.,	57	Yunck & Co.,	60
Winn Boiler Compound,	61	Young, W. C., (gal.,)	79

MISCELLANEOUS INDEX.

	Page.		Page.
Horticultural Hall,	79	Grand Rapids Furniture Pavillion,	84
Art Gallery,	80	Saw-mills,	
Live Stock Stables,		Brick & Drain Tile Machines,	
Electric Railway,		Wagon Sheds,	

Places of Interest in and about New Orleans.

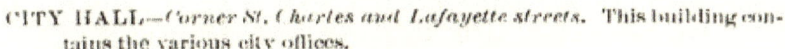

CITY HALL—*Corner St. Charles and Lafayette streets.* This building contains the various city offices.
FRENCH MARKET—*River front, between St. Peter's and Esplanade Streets.* The largest in the South.
U. S. POST-OFFICE AND CUSTOM-HOUSE—*Canal Street, between Decatur and Fulton Streets.* From the top of this building an excellent view of the city can be obtained.
U. S. MINT AND SUB-TREASURY—*Corner Esplanade and North Peters.*
ICE FACTORY—*56 and 62 S. Front Street.* Here can be seen the interesting process of ice-manufacturing.
SUGAR SHEDS—*River Front on Levee, at foot of Bienville, two blocks from Canal Street; down river.*
COTTON EXCHANGE—*Corner Carondelet and Gravier Streets.*

Drives.

1. Up St. Charles Street, passing Lee Place, (monument,) to Washington Avenue.
2. TO CARROLLTON—Up St. Charles Street to Napoleon Avenue, through Napoleon Avenue to river, and up river to Carrollton.
3. NEW LAKE END—Fine drive over shell road, out Canal Street.

Miscellaneous.

JACKSON SQUARE—*Bounded by Chartres, St. Ann, and St. Peter's Streets.* Contains statue of Jackson.
LAFAYETTE SQUARE—*Bounded by Camp, St. Charles, North and South Streets.* Contains statue of B. Franklin.
LEE PLACE—*At intersection of St. Charles and Delord Streets.*
WEST END—Great resort on Lake Ponchartrain, (pronounced Pont' Chartrain'.) Reached by New Shell Road, or by Steam Cars, which leave corner Carondelet and Canal Streets.
SPANISH FORT—Resort on Lake Ponchartrain. Reached by N. O., S. Ft. and Lake R. R.
U. S. BARRACKS—*Down the river.* Take Levee and Barracks Street Car, at foot of Canal Street; or North Rampart and Dauphine Street Car. While at Barracks, take street-car line down the river to Federal Cemetery, which is the place where General Jackson defeated Packenham.

WASHINGTON CEMETERY A novel sight to one unacquainted with New Orleans cemeteries.
OLD FRENCH CEMETERY—*Basin Street, near Canal Street.*
GREENWOOD CEMETERY—*Canal Street.* Take Canal Street Cars.
CARROLLTON GARDENS—A beautiful sight. Take green street-car from Baronne and Canal Streets.
FAIR GROUNDS —Out Canal Street to Broad Street, down Broad to Esplanade Street, up Esplanade to grounds.
UPPER CITY PARK—Includes part of Exposition Grounds 250 acres.
LOWER CITY PARK Fronts on *Metairie road, between old and new canal.*

Information Pertaining to Mardi Gras.

MARDI GRAS (pronounced Marde Graw) means Fat Tuesday—the day before Lent, spent in gayety and festivity. The following are some of the orders which take part: The "Mistic Krew of Comus," organized February 24, 1857; "Rex on Mardi Gras," organized February 13, 1872; "Night Revellers," organized January 6, 1871; "Knights of Momus," organized New Year's Eve, 1872; "Phunny Phorties," organized 1879.

THE WORLD'S INDUSTRIAL AND COTTON CENTENNIAL EXPOSITION

Was originally contemplated as a Cotton Centennial alone, as 1884 was the centennial of the first export of cotton, but was afterwards enlarged in its scope so as to include the various industrial pursuits of the world—hence, denominated as above.

For this the citizens of New Orleans contributed $500,000. State and City, each, $100,000. The United States loaned $1,000,000. U. S. expended on U. S. Building $250,000.

There are Seven Buildings Proper:
1st. MAIN BUILDING—Devoted to general exhibits and Machinery Hall, and is 1,378 - 905 feet, covering 33 acres.
2d. U. S. BUILDING—Devoted to U. S. exhibits, State exhibits, Women's Department, and Colored People's Department. 565 × 885 feet.
3d. HORTICULTURAL HALL, 194 × 600 feet.
4th. MEXICAN BUILDING, 190 - 300 feet.
5th. ART GALLERY, 100 - 250 feet.
6th. FACTORIES AND MILLS -Devoted to exhibits of Cotton in all its stages of manipulation. 150 × 350 feet.
7th. LIVE STOCK STABLES.

Besides these, there are the Mexican Barracks and Grand Rapids (Mich.) Furniture Pavilion, and some smaller buildings, mentioned hereafter.

In Machinery Hall, there are 20 gigantic engines, furnishing 4,200 horse-power.

Before main entrance of principal buildings are two electric lamps of 36,000 candle-power.

The Fountain in Artificial Lake, near Mexican Department, throws jets 100 feet high, illuminated by tower light of 100,000 candle-power.

The music is furnished by the great organ built for the occasion by Pilcher Bros., of New Orleans; Currier's Band, from Cincinnati, composed of fifty musicians, and Prof. F. Widdows, from Washington, D. C., who rings the chimes daily—at noon and evening—and the excellent Mexican Band.

The Park on which the Exposition is situated was one of the oldest plantations under the old Spanish Regime, and special attention is called to the grove of live oaks, extending toward the river, which, by reason of the hanging moss on them, are named "bearded oaks;" notice, also, the ferns growing on the trunks, and that the grass continues its growth right up to the trees.

GENERAL DIRECTIONS

—FOR—

USE OF THIS GUIDE BOOK.

In constructing the Guide, a systematic course has been adopted, and the visitor will find it best to follow its directions, but if it is desired to commence wherever one enters a building, all necessary is to get the name of state, territory, or exhibitor nearest, then, turning to the Index, which is alphabetically arranged, find the page on which the state, territory, or exhibitor is mentioned, and continue as directed. On reaching an exhibit, hastily glance at description in Guide, as in that way you get a better idea of what you wish and are to see.

Separate Indexes have been made for Main and U. S. Buildings, arranged alphabetically, so, with first letter of name of state, territory, or exhibitor, one can turn to that letter in Index and readily find page of Guide where mentioned.

In addition, is a Third or Miscellaneous Index, for other buildings and exhibits, but not arranged alphabetically.

Persons with limited time can hastily look through the Guide and mark that which they particularly wish to see, thus saving the trouble of making a memorandum of it, and then, following directions, go directly to it. Upon examining this book, you will find that taking notes, &c., will be unnecessary, for all principal objects are mentioned and described. In Miscellaneous Index also, may be found location of General Offices and General Exhibits.

UNITED STATES AND STATE EXHIBITS 885x565 feet.

U. S. BUILDING.

For convenience of the viewer, I have divided the first floor of this building into three parts, viz: Right Wing, lying to your right as you enter the Main Entrance, Center, and Left Wing.

The Gallery is divided viz:

Professor Ward's Wonderful Natural History Establishment, over Main Entrance, to the right, and in the end, Colored People's Department: over the Entrance, directly opposite Main Entrance, Women's Department. Next, farther along, Educational Department, which extends to first corner to right of Main Entrance.

The viewer should commence with Iowa, at the right of Main Entrance, then follow the Guide-Book strictly, finishing up the Right Wing first, which contains the Exhibits of the following States and Territories in the order given: Iowa, Minnesota, Nebraska, Dakota, Kansas, Idaho, Washington Territory, Montana Territory, Wyoming, Oregon, New Mexico, Colorado, Arizona, Nevada, California, Illinois, Wisconsin, Indiana, Michigan, Ohio, Connecticut, Vermont, Massachusetts, New Hampshire, Rhode Island, and Maine.

Without examining Center, pass Rear Entrance, to Left Wing, as indicated by Guide-Book, and face Texas Exhibits. In this wing are the following States, viz: Texas, Louisiana, Mississippi, Kentucky, Alabama, Missouri, Georgia, Arkansas, Maryland, Delaware, Pennsylvania, New Jersey, New York, West Virginia, Virginia, North Carolina, South Carolina, and Florida.

Examining the foregoing, as directed by Guide-Book, you reach Florida, which is the last state in Left Wing; here take up Exhibits of General Government, which are shown by following Departments and in following order, viz: Smithsonian Institute, Interior Department, War Department, Treasury Department, State Department, Navy Department, and Post-office.

After examining each division, according to directions, pass upstairs to Women's Department, in Gallery, directly over you; this completed, pass along Gallery to right of Rear Entrance, and you find the Educational Department, which occupies entire gallery to restaurant in end corner, and includes Ward's Natural History Exhibit. Included in this Department are not only the Educational Exhibits of each State, but also Exhibits from The Brothers of the Christian Schools, and from some foreign schools, as shown farther on. At end Gallery, to right of Main Entrance, commences the Colored People's Department, which contains State Representations; passing farther along, you reach the Women's Department, which occupies the side Gallery opposite Main Entrance.

In the Guide, I have called attention to the main features of the respective exhibits, which must be of great assistance, if the Guide be strictly followed.

IOWA.

The exhibit of this state is most creditable and has been arranged with excellent taste. The educational exhibit is in the gallery directly over the state, and will be spoken of in another place. Commence with the display at the wall, where there are a number of charts showing the health condition and social condition of state. These charts are ingeniously constructed and should be carefully studied; next view the vegetable display, which includes 208 varieties of potatoes; next, column of grain, excellent quality; next, the honey exhibit; pyramid of grain and seed, containing 1,500 varieties, with 72 varieties of corn; corn-house, with products of corn inside; see near this, glass globe filled with soil of state; next, wonderful exhibit of flour showing 321 different grades and samples from 91 out of the 99 counties in the state; next, pork; next, their manufacturing exhibit notice in this their fine display of cloths; returning, see geological collection, in which particularly notice mottled marbles, fine specimens of lead ore, one weighing 450 pounds, very pure, and peculiar specimen of pyrites of iron; next, native fruits and woods. The principal exhibit of fruit from this state is at Horticultural Hall.

MINNESOTA.

This state has an area of 83,531 square miles or 58,459,840 acres, is watered by a great number of beautiful lakes. Its surface is undulating and generally presents a landscape of beautiful lawns separated by belts of timber. A considerable portion is covered with timber, and, in addition, upwards of 30,000,000 forest trees have been planted by farmers and are growing. The soil is generally a rich loam, resting on a calcareous substratum. It ranks very high as an agricultural state, particularly for wheat. The north-eastern section is rich in iron and copper ores. For its age, the state is well supplied with manufactures, and its flour manufactures are among the greatest of the world, and its exhibit in this direction is of great interest. Notice especially its wonderful methods and results in manufacturing New Process Flour; ingenious method of filing newspapers, by West Publishing Company; exhibits of granite and gabbro rock, similar to granite but not containing quartz, very fine; representation of "Falls of Minnehaha;" exhibit of birds, animals and minerals, furnished by Prof. W. H. Winchell and the State University; noticeable among the birds is the American Pelican, which makes its home in the state, also a pair of Albino Deer; monument of building stone; exhibit from Pipestone Co., in case; attractive display made in pavilion by Pillsbury Mills, together with process of Flour Making, commencing with specimens of wheat from thresher up to No. 1 New Process Flour, showing 167 different forms. Do not fail to examine the wonderful exhibit of the L. C. Porter Milling Co., of Gluten Flour, varieties of flour, and system of manufacturing and analysis of Graham Flour, and their own manufacture showing the starch and gluten in wheat. Next the Sugar and Syrup exhibit of J. F. Porter, made by his patent process; cabinet of Fish, by Minnesota Fish Commission, showing the native fish, real fish skins stuffed, so as to show the genuine fish.

Prof. Winchell's excellent system of maps, eight in all, showing minerals, topography of land, &c., very interesting.

Indians in Birch bark canoes, with dog sledges, walking in snow shoes, on cotton, to represent snow; also notice Red River Cart, and samples of woods cut down by beavers. That portion of Pipestone Co. where the clay used for making pipes is found has always been considered sacred ground by all Indian

Tribes, and they are all permitted to obtain clay from this place for making "pipes of peace."

Though the Sioux and Chippewa Tribes have always been at enmity, when they meet here they must meet as "friends." Before leaving, do not fail to examine the fine display of flour from the famous Washburn Mills, and excellent building stone, as displayed in stately obelisk.

NEBRASKA.

The area of this state is 75,000 square miles, or 48 million acres, as large as all of New England. It possesses an exceedingly rich soil. Its exhibits are not only numerous and varied, but displayed with so much skill and good taste as to attract the attention of every one. Notice particularly the general features, viz: Bartholdi Statue of "Liberty Enlightening the World," facing a map of U. S. made of different grains; Map, rotary, with the pivotical point Lincoln, Neb.; next, a globe representing the world, with divisions laid off in different grains; the series of large screens on one is the "crowned king," made of kernels of corn. The remainder of this and other screens are artistically ornamented with cut corn. A map of the state covers one screen, showing the number of school-houses and miles of railroad in the state, situation of towns, cities, and post-offices, and the location of all railroad trains at 10 o'clock, A. M., each day; also, settlement of state. On column in front is public-school fund 60 millions dollars; bale of hay of native grass; panel containing 75 varieties of grasses; specimens of tame grasses, with German and French millet around a post; vegetables in rear; Chili squash 216½ pounds in weight - there were 5 of these on one vine, 80 varieties of corn—see these on two posts in front; samples of soil in boxes; stem of blue grass 10 feet in height; specimens of new growth wood, with two varieties of black walnut; samples of finished woods in case, with table of explanation. In front of exhibit new process tanned leather, showing harnesses, whips, &c., made of leather tanned in 12 hours.

DAKOTA.

The exhibit made by this territory is of such a remarkable character as to call particular attention to its domain. The territory is 414 miles long and 316 miles wide, and while adapted to the growth of all cereals, has a large portion of the great wheat and corn belts of the north-west; it has an area of 150,000 square miles—almost three times as large as the great state, New York. The mound which you first see, covered with rocks, petrified woods, animals, &c., is intended to represent the territory as it was when found by the white settlers. The display of woods is not made so much to indicate that the territory is now rich in wood, but what its soil could produce, and what they believe was once plentiful, but destroyed by fires. Of the animals, notice particularly Moose, on front of mound; White Buffalo, at right, very scarce, cost $1,000; pair of American Antelopes, in rear of mound, distinguished by his black horns; Rocky Mountain Sheep, distinguished by his large horns. Turning from these to the log-cabin, at right, see the large Buffalo Wolf, or Loafer, as he is called, which is a cross with the dog; Prairie

Wolf, or Coyote, which is allied to the dog species; beautiful display of mounted animal heads, and mirrors ornamented with horns; pair of antler's heads, with horns locked as, it is said, they locked during a fight, thus causing their death. Mr. W. L. Barrows, of Mandam, Da., owner of the cabin and display, has also interesting Indian relics, together with photographs illustrative of the Custer Massacre. He displays, too, some wonderful petrifications: ask to see petrified heart of buffalo.

Turning back to state exhibit, examine a box of Jasper Granite, found at Sioux Falls, and is being used quite generally for building: also, round stones, resembling cannon balls, which give name to Cannon Ball river, in the Devil Lake Region; Indian carved stones; wonderful grain column; native grasses, six feet high, from bottom-lands, and three to four feet high from uplands; tame grasses and millets: display of grain; flour manufactured in the Territory; special attention is called to soil exhibits, showing a depth of seven feet in bottom-lands, and three to four feet in uplands: a loam soil, said to be easily worked. The population of this territory is now fully 500,000, large railroad facilities, flourishing business towns, great agricultural resources and development, excellent schools, and yet is deprived of the privilege and rights of state government. Is not this deprivation a great injustice?

KANSAS.

This state has an area of upwards of 52,000,000 acres, and an analysis shows its soil to be among the best in the world, and has demonstrated it to be, perhaps, the best wheat soil in the world. In 1883 its average wheat production was nearly 23 bushels to the acre, and about the same in 1884. Its display here is very attractive. Notice particularly, as follows, viz: The monument Ceres —you will have to take a position some distance in the rear to properly view it; the name of state, "Kansas," a beautiful oil painting -this and the monument "Ceres" are the work of Mr. A. Rohe, of Lawrence, Kansas; several varieties of corn, on ears 15 inches long; map showing schools, railroads, towns, post-offices, &c.; number of school-children, 382,986; number of school-houses, 6,299, and number of teachers, 8,423; see 120 varieties of small canned fruit; immense strawberries, running 25 to the quart, a new variety, called the "Surprise;" near Ceres, columns of grains; silk exhibit, showing in forms from cocoon to ribbon, made in State; case of 63 varieties of evaporated fruits, prepared by one Kansas farmer; fruit evaporators; case containing all varieties of native woods; flour exhibit, claimed to be superior to Minnesota flour; corn in stalk, 18 feet high; mineral specimens, lead and zinc, southeast Kansas, a mineral region; millets, 7 feet high; cotton, and hemp, 16 feet high; building stone; beautiful brooms, made in this state. Upon leaving this state, before viewing Idaho, examine the exhibit of C. M. and St. P. R. R.

As you leave the Kansas exhibit from rear, you reach the remarkable exhibit of C. M. and St. P. R. R., which includes largely Dakota exhibits. The grain lady was made by the ladies of Aberdeen, Dakota. The small locomotive—"The Alexander Mitchell"—was made by the ladies of Mitchell, Dakota. The railroad train was made at Aberdeen, Dakota, by William Sibben, who, with Mr. Powell, designed the exquisite wheat structure before you. Notice particularly exhibits of Wisconsin woods, Dakota vegetables, including a pumpkin weighing 185 pounds, a squash weighing 146 pounds, a case of fine minerals, and Indian relics of Sitting Bull's tribe. From this exhibit go to Idaho, in the regular order.

IDAHO.

Though this territory is mountainous, it has 40,000,000 acres adapted to grazing, and includes large areas adapted to agriculture. It abounds in many valuable timbers, such as pine, fir, and red cedar. Its vegetable display is not large, but creditable, showing potatoes weighing seven pounds each, a pumpkin weighing 140 pounds. The greatest display of the territory is exhibitions of its mineral resources. Notice particularly, as follows, viz: Gold and silver bricks, weighing 50 pounds each, and a number of bars of silver; specimens from the Ramshorn mine, Custer county, of block sulphates, gray copper, and native silver, which assays from $200 to $5,000 per ton—width of vein six feet—sold for $500,000; from Barclay Galena mine, 67 per cent. lead and $127 per ton silver—width of vein four feet; from Viola mine, 76 per cent. lead, 137 ounces per ton silver—richest lead mine in United States—a thirty-foot vein without waste; from Minnie Moore mine, black sulphates and gray copper, averages $250 silver per ton—sold for half a million; specimens from the Custer mine in case examine them; this mine keeps thirty stamping-mills running, and has paid for everything and has left one and three fourths millions; specimens from Excelsior mine, Custer county very rich and immense; specimens from Montana mine, Custer county, first 300 tons of ore taken, assayed $1,000 per ton; specimens from Silver Wing mine, Custer county—thought to be the richest mine in United States—averages $1,000 per ton; specimens from Atlanta mine, $2,000 per ton—very extensive—see ruby silver in specimens; they claim to show you the richest specimens of gold quartz in the world; from Mother Lode mine, weighs 1,055 pounds, valued at $10,000—ask to see it—96 nuggets visible, besides trace gold; next see a pair of deer-horns with a foot growing out of them; a pair of Rocky Mountain sheep horns, each horn measuring twenty-one inches in circumference; see oil painting of Shoshone Falls, on Snake river.

WASHINGTON TERRITORY.

The territory has an area of 42,803,200 acres. That part of the territory west of the Colorado Range is densely wooded. The climate is similar to that of England. The soil is very rich. One of the most remarkable features of the exhibits is its display of timber, and should be thoroughly examined by every man interested in that direction. Notice particularly as follows, viz: A fir-tree plank 24 x 4¼ feet; a transverse cut, from a fir tree over 6 feet in diameter; white ash; 24 varieties of polished woods; specimens of grains, including wheat and remarkable oats; fine samples of potter's clay and brick; specimens of grasses; samples from its fisheries; specimens of work of Neah Bay Indians; vegetables, including potatoes weighing 8 pounds and a squash weighing 216 pounds; specimens of gold, silver, and copper ores.

MONTANA.

This territory contains an area of 143,776 square miles, or 92,000,000 acres. Although the main range of the Rocky Mountains extends through the territory, yet its valleys are exceedingly rich in fertile soil and vegetation. It also possesses millions of acres of rich meadow land. The territory's greatest wealth lies in the extent and richness of her mines of, principally, gold, silver, copper, and lead, and its exhibits consist mainly of specimens of these minerals, in order that she may attract the attention of capitalists to the opportunities offered for paying investments. Notice, in particular, specimen of mineral rock from "Moulton" mine, worth $2,000 per ton, or $1 per pound; specimen of "Queen's Hill" lode, which yields 150 ounces of silver per ton of ore; specimen from "Drum Lummond" mine, worth $800 per ton—this vein is 80 feet wide, very remarkable; specimen from "Montana View" lode, very rich in copper—owners have refused half a million dollars for it; specimen from "Gregory Consolidated" mine, 60 per cent. lead, and yields 800 ounces of silver per ton; specimens of rock containing silver and copper together; specimen from "Gloster" gold mine, in which is to be seen $3,700 in gold - the mine has already produced $1,000,000; specimens of lead and silver bullion; method of reducing ores, as illustrated; process for reducing copper ores.

WYOMING.

This territory makes a rich, rare, and curious display, and its exhibits are very complete, consisting of coal, samples of gold, silver, tin, and copper ores, ten varieties of petroleum, game, birds, fossil fish, alabaster, and collection of curiosities, and photographs of "Yellowstone National Park." Notice, particularly, as follows, viz: Specimen of carbonate of soda, (of which they possess a lake;) sulphate of soda, (of which they have 320 acres;) kaolin, (of which there is a large deposit;) specimens of granite and white and black marbles; petroleum; mica; epsom salts, (of which they possess a lake;) sulphur, (of which there is a mountain;) asbestos; gold, silver, and copper ores; remarkable specimen showing silver in limestone; wonderful geode—don't fail to see—case of fine agates.

Case of hot water formation; section of petrified tree; case of sulphur crystals; hematite iron, used for paint; specimen of iron mountain, and also photograph; case of fish and other interesting fossils; Indian collection; case of formations in Yellowstone Springs; a wonderful photograph rock, on which is a sun picture; angora wool, from goat which makes the territory its home.

OREGON.

This state, though traversed by two ranges of mountains—the Coast range and Cascade range, continuations of the Sierras—possesses a rich soil in its valleys, and its plains are highly productive of wheat and some other cereals; the wheat is unusually good. The state's exhibit speaks in the strongest language of its richness of soil, its mild climate, its great fertility of soil, and remarkable degree of healthfulness make the State vastly important, and especially to those seeking homes. Notice particularly, as follows, viz: Oil painting of "Mt. Hood," by Stewart, hanging on rear wall. The view is taken from a point showing crater, and is an excellent piece of art; it is valued at $1,000. Near this picture are specimens of most beautifully etched touchwood, 42 varieties of wheat, some of which yielded 64 bushels to the acre, with straw measuring 1½ inches in circumference and 6 feet in length; oats 7 feet high, with heads 16 inches long, yielding 162 bushels to the acre; rye 7 feet high; 37 varieties of grasses, including timothy 7 feet high, corn with stalks nearly 19 feet high, rutabagas weighing 58 pounds, turnips 39 pounds, cabbage 41 pounds, potato 8½ pounds, onions 16½ inches in circumference, radishes 10 inches in diameter, carrots 32 inches long, hops growing 2,300 pounds to the acre. Its remarkable collection of woods used in manufacturing, including beautiful specimens of the wavy maple, burl (knot) maple, and myrtle; almonds, case of minerals, specimens of manufactures.

Richmond and Danville R. R. System.

The exhibit made by this railroad system, for variety of useful and rich mineral ores and timber, is certainly wonderful. This system extends from Alexandria, Va., to Birmingham, Ala., through Virginia to Charlotte, N. C., where the road branches, one line going to Augusta, Ga., the other extending through Atlanta, Ga., to Birmingham, Ala., and its display is collected from along its line. It includes rich specimens of gold ore which sells at the mine for $125 per ton. This rich deposit extends along the line of road 400 miles in the form of sulphides, free milling and placer varieties. Attention is called to the rich exhibit of silver and lead, copper, iron in every form, among which are the rich Bessemer ores, and an ore out of which steel equaling that of Damascus Blades is made, manganese, zinc, quartz, feldspar and mica for porcelain, kaolin, soapstone, granite, and many other minerals. Notice particularly the collection of precious gems, including emeralds, rubies, &c., gold nuggets, N. C. diamonds, quartz, amethysts, &c., all in cases back of tables containing minerals; also, back of these, among the 150 varieties of woods, see Gopher wood, finished curly maple and cherry lumber. The mineral and wood resources from which these specimens are procured are said to exist in the greatest abundance, and I understand that this display is in part made to show the world the vast resources of the country through which this system of railroad passes. Next exhibit is a part of the collection of this same system, from Birmingham, Ala., including principally coal and iron; one specimen of coal weighs 26,000 pounds. Capt. C. C. McPhail is in charge of these exhibits and willingly imparts any information desired concerning them.

East Tennessee and Virginia R. R.

On entering this exhibit, notice particularly the fine display of Tennessee marbles and several varieties taken from same quarry, and in large piece on table, next to rear aisle, is illustrated how these changes occur; among woods, notice section of immense beech tree and fine cherry lumber, and with iron and coal exhibit, section of tree which has been coked. Mr. C. H. War ing has charge of this exhibit, and very kindly furnishes any desired information. Leaving this exhibit, you next examine New Mexico.

NEW MEXICO.

This territory is making an exceedingly novel and attractive display, including a cave, so constructed as to represent stalactites hanging within, back of which is a mirror, which, in the electric light reflects the stalactites, precious minerals, and fine display of wines, scattered effectively around ; within the cave will also be found wonderful specimens of copper ore, and rude step-ladders, mining-baskets, mining-tools, &c., used in silver-mining by the Aztecs, which were excavated 300 feet below the surface. In front of cave are photographs of Indian students of Albuquerque, accompanied by their work ; crossing aisle, notice display made by Billing's Smelting Works, of bullion and ore, of gold, silver, and copper ; the large display of ore on the left is from Socorro county ; upon the ore, just mentioned at the corner, is a dummy representing a "prospector;" much of the ore displayed is very rich, assaying $1,200 per ton. The bags contain carbonate silver sand, and should be carefully examined, for it is very beautiful ; back of this see petrified wood ; also large and small century plants; the small one was obtained 13,000 feet above sea level, for this Exposition, to secure certainty of its blooming this year; notice flower and stalks of century plant, 16 feet high, indicating the peculiar way this plant blossoms; to the right, see large collection of minerals from Lincoln county, containing very rich ores, assaying $3,000 per ton, pyramid of genuine Blosburg coal and coke made from it ; on top of coal, petrified timber; next pyramid and table containing agricultural productions, medicinal and dyeing plants; see corn 15 feet high. with seven ears on one stalk ; soap plant, which is actually used for laundry purposes; wild hops, good for use ; Senora wheat, very peculiar ; Mexican beans, from which the celebrated Mexican cakes are made; examine fruits, raisins, and nuts, plums, and nectarines especially, also samples of 62 kinds of grasses and millet, nearly all raised from 6,000 to 8,000 feet above sea level ; while here examine black wheat, wild rye, and oats, and very near observe enormous sweet potatoes, some weighing 18 pounds ; and near there, notice large leather cask, which the Mexicans use in making wine; at end of table, in Lincoln county display, notice particularly the wonderful "forest rocks." These rocks are beautifully painted by the hand of Nature, and if they are wet with water you will see the picture most effectively brought out. The blankets on exhibition were made by Indians; notice also, Indian tanned sheep and goat skins. The angora wool display ; the birds you see are mountain quails; cases of Grant county ore, some of the specimens assaying $20,000 for gold per ton ; see bags of lentils; at rear of Socorro county exhibit, notice the celebrated Mexican adobe brick, of which Mexican houses are built, and near these fire-proof stone and marble; on next table beyond, in Santa Fe county, mineral exhibit, see wonderful petrifactions and honey-comb sand, in which the bees make their honey. On returning to the aisle, observe ruins of old Spanish church, for which building materials were brought from Spain. Leaving this, enter Colorado, commencing with agricultural display, in alcove.

COLORADO.

There is so much of interest in this exhibit that I can only call attention to the leading features. Notice particularly as follows, viz: Remarkable agricultural display in alcove, from State Agricultural College, of wheat from Palestine, barley and rye from every nation in the world, Chinese oats that are hulless, fall wheat changed from spring wheat, native grasses, second crop of oats from one sowing. The whiteness of straw is by reason of no rain. In this alcove is also work in wood and iron, done by students; and towards front is the private mineral collection of Mr. J. G. Heistand, of Manitou Springs Co., including nuggets of silver, worth $60, topaz on amazon stone, fine gold quartz, native jet, moss agates, &c., &c. This exhibit is for sale. The mineral ore near this collection is much of it very rich, assaying $3,000 per ton. Next back in cabinet is a model showing a silver mine, its shafts, chambers, pumping works, &c., and in large chamber miners at work. Next back is miner's cabin, built of mineral ores, and contains fine specimens from all parts of the state, and manufactured goods. The mineral exhibit of state is divided among counties, and after leaving the cabin you come to Gilpin Co., which is the Pike's Peak Region. Here the silver and gold obelisk shows the silver and gold taken from this district. The base, 8 feet square and 5 feet high, represents in size the quantity and value of silver, $5,000,000. The gold, 5 feet square at base, is 10 feet high and 2 feet square at top, and represents in size and value the gold taken, $15,000,000. This county also shows rich gold and silver ores, and a rounded boulder taken out 270 feet down in solid rock. Just beyond this in background is grand and very natural-looking Colorado and Rocky Mountain scenery, the left side of which displays the Royal Gorge and Grand Cañon of the Arkansas river, whose walls are 3,000 feet high, and illustration of the passing through of a Denver and Rio Grande R. R. train. In distant background are seen Snow Range peaks, which are covered with perpetual snow. The Mount of the Holy Cross. This cross is 300 feet high, formed by chasms in mountain side. Also Pike's Peak, the highest point in the world inhabited by man, showing the signal station 14,200 feet above sea level. In front of the mountains is a miniature landscape, illustrating farming by irrigation. See reservoir and different methods of irrigation. Next, notice Leadville exhibit of ores; very fine. Next, Chaffe Co. exhibit from 200 mines, rich gold, silver, and copper ores, some assaying $2,000 per ton. See gold brick and silver bullion. Next, Gunnison Co. mine, notice anthracite coal; varieties of building stone; rich gold and silver ores from various mines; fine specimen from Excelsior mine, showing chloride of silver; gold ore from Gold Cup mine, assaying $2,000 per ton. Back of this, Pitkin Co. See specimens of silver bullion. Ore from Span mine, which has produced $2,000,000 last year. In front of Gunnison Co., statistics of production, and collection of mineral specimens in cases of Span Aspen and Vellejho mines. Returning, notice views of Leadville in 1877 and 1884, and statistics of mineral products for 6 years, from 1878 to 1884, inclusive, giving total of 97 millions. In going towards next exhibit, Arizona, see exhibit of Clear Creek Co., where the first discovery of silver was made in the state. This mining territory, 15 miles long and 6 miles wide, has produced 30 millions of dollars. Notice statistics on panels of this and Grande Co., back of exhibit.

ARIZONA.

This territory has an area of 114,000 square miles, or 72,000,000 of acres. Though much of the territory is mountainous, still large portions of it are rich in agricultural and grazing lands. The mining interests are as yet in the infancy of their development; but discoveries at Tombstone, Tucson, and other points have demonstrated their richness. Since the opening of the S. P. R. R., it has taken a high rank in the production of minerals. Cochise is probably the richest mining county in the territory. Should there have been any doubts as to the wealth of the territory in this direction, its display here will certainly remove them. Commencing where the exhibit joins California, notice, particularly, as follows, viz: Large display of copper ore from the Dominion mine, Globe district, which is the richest copper mine in the territory; also, great variety of copper and rich horn silver ores from same mine; next three exhibits include large specimens from Queen mine, the largest weighing 7,325 pounds, 25 per cent copper; specimens surrounding this mass of copper from 50 different mines; large cube of copper weighing 1,100 pounds. The rocks on this cube indicate the character of rock lying above the copper. Next see collection of ore from Yavapaia county, including copper with gold and silver and bullion, 96 per cent. of copper and $290 gold and silver; pyramid of silver and gold ore from Cochise county, running from $40 to $4,000 per ton, with lead and silver bullion. Turning to right, the first case of mineral shows the changes in ore as it passes through the process of smelting. The next case contains Tombstone ore of lead and free gold; also, specimens of fire-clay, and free gold on it. The third case contains ores from Pima county, and represents all the varieties of ore in the territory, and should be carefully studied. See among it gold and silver nuggets, Arizona diamond, many native reptiles and insects, including the Gila monster, skin of rattlesnake 40 feet long, tarantalus and centipedes in bottles. In this case is also a fine specimen of green copper, or malachite, and cerusite, or crystallized carbonate of lead. The next cases contain rich silver ores from Casa Grande district. The last case in row contains rich gold and silver ores from Globe district. Turning about and taking cases on the other side, you find rich silver ores from Pima county. The best exhibit of the territory is contained in the high velvet-lined cases at your right. This collection is worth $20,000 for bullion alone, and is from the Silver King mine, Pinal county, and is one of the finest exhibits at the exposition. It contains a kind of silver unequaled in the world. Back of this, and next Colorado space, is the fine collection of mineral specimens of Prof. C. R. Wores, including 2,500 specimens remarkable for rarity and richness; and also the most novel feature of the exhibit, which is a collection of petrified or silicified wood from what is known as the petrified forest of Apache county, Arizona. No other state can produce such a novelty. In the rear of exhibit see case of vanadimite and wulfernite, which is lead crystallized, from Uma county. See also mountain sheep, exhibit of wheat, fruits, apples, pomegranates, honey, and Indian pottery; an excellent kind of tanning material, produced from a weed which grows abundantly in the desert; display of sugar cane and cotton from Salt River valley, Mariposa county; quite an interesting feature, for it is not generally known that Arizona could produce these articles.

NEVADA.

This state makes a commendable display of agricultural and horticultural products, showing fine potatoes and apples—of latter, notice beautiful rosy-cheeked lady apples. The principal feature of its exhibit is the wonderful collection of minerals and photographs relating to mining interests. The display includes several private cabinets, among which are those belonging to Senator Jones, Mr. J. Shaw, S. Dowling, W. M. Havener; also the state exhibit and that of the Pacific Coast Pioneers. Specimens of ore are shown which assay $20,000 per ton. Notice particularly, as follows, viz: Gold nuggets from rocks which yielded $100,000 per ton; silver ore, worth $21,000 per ton; gold leaf; specimens showing gold, silver, copper, and mercury together; granulations of gold and silver ores from the Comstock mine. See following petrifactions: Bird's-nest with eggs in it; piece of fence-post with a nail in it; sandstone with wedge in it, which has petrified within last eight years; see, also, casts showing elephant's tracks, tooth, and tusk; a man's foot 22 inches long; these were found in sand 40 feet below the surface. See photographs of prominent mines, and original drawings of great Sutro Tunnel, 8 miles in length and from 8 to 16 feet in diameter, driven inside of mountain at a depth of 1,600 feet, to drain the great mines. The product of the Nevada mines has already been $500,000,000. Carefully examine each of the collections, as they are very fine and rich: in fact, the entire state exhibit will repay the closest examination.

CALIFORNIA.

Commencing near wall of the building with botanical display, which is very large and fine, proceed towards center, and see case in which is a pair of gloves made of a woman's skin; next, beautiful column of borax; near this, section of first big tree discovered, (1853,) cut 100 feet from butt, and measuring 17 feet in diameter, lies flat on floor, and near it is its bark, 39 inches thick; at right, section of immense pine tree; farther on, section of red wood tree; next, the honey exhibit, methods of extracting same—five southern counties of the state produced 10,000 tons of honey during last year; also the white sage honey, made from white sage bush, of which see specimen; to left, National Grange exhibit, in which is ostrich eggs, beet weighing 81 pounds, and sweet potatoes 39 pounds; remarkable grasses and grains, and near them specimen of the Yucca Draconis tree, used for making fibrous material—read card of explanation; next, on right, table of remarkable vegetables, and lemon tree, near by, bearing fruit; table of fruits; next, beyond this, squash weighing 222 pounds; to right, table of vegetables and grains; to left, San Joaquin county exhibit, with silk display, and near, model of Centennial harvester, which cuts, threshes, and sacks forty acres of wheat a day; next, Sacramento county, which is included in the Southern Pacific exhibit; next, toward Arizona, is Sonora county; next, Yola county exhibit, in which see remarkable one year's growth of black walnut; near Nevada county exhibit, see immense grape vine; continuing onward, examine wood display, in which see yellow and sugar pine, red wood plank 6¼ feet wide, polished woods, including a burl (knot) of red wood, and case of polished woods made into sleeve-buttons, &c. California is the leading seed-producing state in the Union, and shows, from one firm, 640 different samples of grain seed; notice, particularly, bunch of peanuts as they grow; palm leaf stripped and made into basket and hat; cotton, grains, wines, nuts, Japanese persimmons, and attractive display of canned fruits; mineral display of gold, silver, and copper ores, and private mineral cabinet worth $10,000; samples of beet-sugar; interesting photographic views of mining interests and native scenery.

Leaving this state, pass directly to Illinois and view exhibit as directed.

ILLINOIS.

The exhibit of this state, in many respects, is quite different from others. Its University makes a wonderful display in manufactures of wood and iron, mechanical engineering, architectural drawing and structure, and specimens of free-hand drawing and design. Commencing at the side of building, notice particularly, as follows, viz: Illustrations of live stock; in alcove at right, around the walls, is work of the schools of Aurora, Ills., that at farther side is of beginners, and in front that of the High School; on panels of this room or alcove, outside, is the art work of the Industrial University, which is very creditable and deserves careful examination: on this wall are two excellent paintings, by Jean Smith, of Chicago, entitled "The Post" and "The Finish." The grand stair and bridges are work of the University Students, also the wood and iron work in cases to the right: the viewer will find in case mechanism representing all forms of motion; next, on right, are cases of native wood; next, on right, is a case containing one of the most interesting exhibits of the state—the analysis of every cereal, with every property contained in the cereal surrounding it, so that the viewer can see for himself what food is composed of and which is most nutritive, &c.; farther along and in center is a collection of seeds and grain; farther back is an octagon pagoda, which cost $1,000, showing resources of state; in the rear are pillars of salt and coal; next, wool exhibit; photographs showing Chicago burned and rebuilt, and other scenery in the state; the Lincoln and Douglas monuments; fine map exhibit by Rand, McNally & Co.; at side of exhibit are models and specimens of manufacturing, including the "bed of roses," specimens of clay, including tile and brick made therefrom, and specimens from Economic Geology in cases, including building stones; near center of exhibit, display of native woods—notice group entitled "Childhood's Palmy Days," designed by E. E. Wood, Esq., Assistant Commissioner; next, see instruments of cruelty to animals, collected by the Illinois Humane Society.

WISCONSIN.

The object of this state is to show its resources, and therefore exhibits minerals, cereals, vegetables, fruits, dairy products, woods, cloths, and leather. Commencing nearest the wall of building, you find the display of excellent woods; next, on left, is cheese and butter display; in 3d case on left, potatoes; 4th case, sugars and articles manufactured from them—see here sorghum flour; 5th case, tobacco and vegetables; 6th case, fruits; 7th case, honey—

notice here the process of preventing honey from crystallizing by heating to 130 degrees; 8th case, seeds, including 73 varieties of bean seeds; 9th and 10th cases, flour, and wheat from which it is made; 11th and 12th cases, varieties of wheat labeled; 13th, 14th, 15th, and 16th cases, fine flint corn; on returning to left, see manufactures, each case complete, from a different mill; cases of fleece and samples of wool, fleece weighing as much as 35 pounds; in last large case is a portion of the Women's Exhibit, which contains many beautiful and interesting articles, among which notice, on small boat, a piece of flag from Sir John Franklin's ship; variety of needle-work and painting, including crimson plush altar cloth, linen lace lambrequin, table and piano covers, sofa pillow embroidered in poppies, doylies, screen; case containing hand-painted china, three plates and beautiful wood inlaying and mosaic work by Mrs. Alexander Mitchell. Farther along is the school exhibit, charts showing statistics of public schools; work of inmates of blind asylum; on other side, map of state up to date—notice what it shows. Leaving this state, enter Indiana nearest wall.

INDIANA.

When it is known that the commissioner and his assistants have labored in making this wonderful display without any state appropriation, and that what has been accomplished has been by individual enterprise, it must be a matter of surprise, for the exhibit is such now as to be commended on all hands. The head-quarters are tastefully arranged, and contain fine portraits of Governor Porter and Governor-elect Gray, and fine oil paintings by Miss Eva Stein, of Lafayette, Ind., and farther on will be adorned with a $1,000 bed-room set. Commencing at the state house, notice particularly, as follows, viz: The beautiful encaustic tile display, made of Indiana clay at Indianapolis; moving back, see panels covered with native grasses and grains; the White county collection of corn; Sugar Valley Seed Company's exhibit; Gibson county grain and vegetable exhibit; display of goods from the Evansville Cotton and Woolen Mills; kaolin, and china made from it; cases of Indian relics, including tools and farming implements; display of nuts and honey; model of the Quaker Brick Machine, with process of manufacture; new style of wire fence which surrounds head-quarters—only made in this state; display of coal, including cannel coal; excellent collection of woods; see on back wall illustrations showing the three capitols which the state has had, and notice improvements, the third and last costing $2,500,000.

MICHIGAN.

This state exhibits her resources in substantial and staple products of which she stands at the head. As you enter the space, you are at once made aware of the fact by banners suspended from a very tasty railing inclosing the entire exhibit, twisted with blue, from which is suspended a banner upon which very full statistics are given of population, area in square miles, acres of land, farm products, farming lands, mineral statistics, value of products, &c. Entering space next to wall, you find the educational exhibit, which is very complete, showing the graded system of education of Michigan. The free-school system, including the primary, the agricultural college, and the University, which can be entered by any one without any charge of tuition; you will here see pupil's work from the first year and grade, on through each year and grade, to and through the high school, into and through the University, where he receives his "sheep skin," entitling him to all the rights and privileges of a gentleman and scholar. To the left, is the elegant forestry display, among which is the Agricultural College collection, very complete and properly classified, showing every variety and family of the native woods, giving the largest variety of any state in the Union, comprising over 800 samples. The collection of M. Engelman, of Manistee county, shows over 400 samples; 13 panels from H. George & Son, of Detroit, made of native woods, as they are used for interior decoration. Imitation in panels for cabinet work, made by the Veneer and Panel Company, and the Plumb & Lewis Manufacturing Company of Grand Rapids. Large sections of trees and planks from various lumber companies through the State. In center of space is one of the most complete and tastefully arranged cereal displays in the Government Building, showing the varieties of native grain. This is an entirely original idea of Mr. Noble, the general manager in charge, to concentrate much into little space, and at the same time give information regarding the resources of the state in general. Passing on, you enter the mineral display, where you will see a pyramid of jugs, containing mineral water from the "Owen Well," Ypsilanti, a very fine display; a can from Mt. Clement's mineral springs; a pyramid of salt forms one of the conspicuous displays from the Michigan Salt Association, showing one of the valuable resources of the state. Passing this, you are surrounded on all sides by minerals—copper from all the mines of Lake Superior, in rock, mass, ingot, bar, and plate, and its various forms of manufacture, as shown by the Detroit Copper and Brass Rolling-mill. The Lake Superior slate in different forms as prepared for market. This slate is superior to any slate yet discovered, as it is susceptible of perfect cleavage in any size or thickness; to right, fine display of iron ores from all the large mines of the Marquette and Menomine iron range; valuable cabinet specimens of copper, iron, gypsum, &c., make this an interesting section of the exhibit. A pyramid of gypsum, also the manufacture of same into an article largely in demand now for paint or calcium, called "alabastine," or diamond finish, which comes prepared in all colors, ready to mix with water, for use. Passing on, you have to your right the potato exhibit, which contains over 600 varieties, the largest number in the United States. Michigan stands at the head in staple products: "1st" in copper; "1st" in iron-ore and charcoal pig-iron; "1st" in forestry and lumber; "1st" in salt; "1st" in fresh water fisheries; "4th" in wool; "4th" in quantity, but "1st" in quality of wheat, and "1st" in apples, of all the States in the Union.

Michigan may well feel proud of her resources, and of the way they are represented to the public for examination, so that he who runs may read. Pass from this State into Ohio.

OHIO.

The exhibits of this state comprise a large display of agricultural products, including 140 varieties of wheat, 20 cases of mound builders' remains, 32 cases of wool, 20 cases of fleece, 12 cases of samples wood, cabinets native woods, specimens representing geology of state, maps illustrating geology, history, archaeology, Indian mounds, railroads, and topography, women's work, 4 cases of art pottery from Cincinnati, carved wood work and hammered brass, by Cincinnati School of Design, fruit display, educational display, and an apiary of 100 swarms, outside near the Government Building.

Commencing at Commissioner's Office, next to wall of building, notice, particularly, as follows, viz: Carved work of Cincinnati School of Design; women's work; art; next, geological collection; next, agricultural display, including wheat, oats, corn, and grasses—carefully examine; in center, pagoda of grains; next, mill products of grains; collection of native woods; specimens of wool, in fleece, and samples, with photographs of the sheep from which they were taken; display of vegetables, with which is women's domestic department, showing fruits preserved a very fine display; see, also, glass globes, 74 inches in height, manufactured by Quaker City Window Glass Co., Quaker City, Ohio; see on wall, next to Michigan Department, illustrations of school-houses. Leaving this exhibit, turn to your left, and enter Connecticut.

CONNECTICUT.

Entering this state from Ohio, you find its exhibit made up largely of manufactured goods. Notice, particularly, case containing busts in clay of Tennyson's "Merlin and Vivian," also bust of Gov. Buckingham, both by E. S. Woods, of Hartford, Conn.; case of fine cutlery, including a knife with 35 blades; case, under clock, of plated and porcelain ware, fine silk and merino hosiery; brass goods; in case near this, exquisite display of tapestry goods in raw silk, embroidered in gold tinsel; fine display of novelty work; geological curiosities from celebrated "brown stone" quarries of Connecticut Valley. You next visit Vermont, entering nearest to state-house.

VERMONT.

Though this state was late in getting her exhibit in its space and arranged, yet it is making a display which attracts universal attention and interest. The state house, of itself, is an ornament, made of native woods, containing a kitchen of "an hundred years ago," and alongside of it a modern kitchen; it has a beautiful slate roof, with name of state in red letters. In front of this house is an arch of marble and granite 17 feet high, 16 feet wide, and 7 feet deep, in imitation of the "Arch of Titus" in Rome. Notice particularly, great variety and excellent quality of slate, including specimens 6–15 feet; among woods, see beautiful bird's-eye maple and veneers, including birch veneering from which furniture is made; excellent display of marbles; fine dairy display; celebrated Barnard panther, weighing 200 pounds, and a bear weighing over 200 pounds. Next enter Massachusetts.

MASSACHUSETTS.

The exhibit of this state is designed to show principally the educational and charitable institutions, and her industrial resources, art-work, fisheries, minerals, and especially building stone. Commencing next to New Hampshire, notice particularly collection of relics loaned by Benjamin Perley Poore, Esq., 3 British muskets, captured in the Revolution; 1 Continental Light infantry musket, 1 French musket, 1 Captain's pike, Revolutionary; 1 Lieutenant's half pike, Revolutionary; 1 Sergeant's halberd, Revolutionary; Alexander Hamilton's camp-kettle, used by him while on Washington's staff; General Knox's saddle, Watchman's hook, containing a sword; Watchman's rattle, 2 Bayonne daggers, (original bayonet,) 4 Continental bayonets, 1 Continental cartridge-box, smoking tongs, pewter bowl and spoon, for bean porridge; 4 pewter porringers, 2 pewter plates, Colonial rapier, Turkish scimitor, 2 French rapiers, sword carried at Bunker Hill, John Randolph's pocket pistol, Revolutionary cartridge-box, British officer's sword, pistols of Captain Key, author of "Star Spangled Banner;" General Wolf's pocket-book, Lafayette's Masonic collar and gloves, General Knox's shoe-buckles, worn at Washington's inauguration; Samuel Adam's shoe-buckles, 6 Continental newspapers, and Continental money. Turning to left, in alcove, notice display of Chelsea Art Casting Company, consisting of bronze plaques, armour, mantles, and fancy articles; in next alcove, display of Prang & Co., of Boston, justly celebrated for their chromos, cards of every description, &c.; and the Photo-Engraving Company, Estes & Lauriat, Heliotype Printing Company, and others; here is shown new processes of photo-etching, lithographing, and reproduction of art-work by recasting; art-work of Industrial School; art-work of Massachusetts Normal School; and further along, industrial exhibit of Massachusetts School for the Feeble-Minded; see on wall near this, map of statistics of state and her schools; table of minerals, including building stone; next, the fisheries; on other side of partition a dory, or fish boat, equipped for halibut fishing; also Low's Life Saving Service. Read card on it. Proceed from this exhibit to New Hampshire.

NEW HAMPSHIRE.

The exhibit from this state consists largely in textile fabrics from several different factories, principally at Manchester. Notice particularly as follows, viz: A profile map of state, (lying flat,) representing the mountains, rivers, and valleys; fine samples of woolen blankets; case of fine worsted goods; blackboard made of soapstone; case of native woods; apple machines; wonderful invalid bed, which should be carefully examined; shearing machine; case showing wonderful exhibit of foxes, birds, &c. Don't fail to notice. Also, very fine specimens of granite, placed on low columns. This is the finest granite displayed at the Exposition. From this state you pass into Rhode Island.

RHODE ISLAND.

The exhibit of this state embraces three sections: 1st. Educational. 2d. National Products. 3d. Manufactured Products. The educational consists of examinations, drawing, penmanship, carving and clay-molding, maps, and charts, showing number and grades and government of schools, work from School of Design, free-hand and mechanical drawing, photographs of Educational Buildings. Notice particularly the maps and charts of school statistics, photographs of school-houses, and specimens of free-hand and mechanical drawing.

The natural products consist of animals, birds, shell fish, reptiles, minerals, and woods. Notice particularly the collection of birds in the center: specimens of various woods, with leaves and autumn foliage.

The manufactured products are largely represented in Main Building, but here are represented Jewelry Industry of Providence, cotton and woolen industry, paper-making from wood, and iron novelty manufacture. Notice particularly excellent cotton and woolen goods, paper made from wood, and stove used on Greely Expedition, made by Barston Stove Co. Next enter Maine, which finishes the Right Wing.

MAINE.

This state makes a very interesting display, which does great credit to itself and the Commissioner. You will see much here that you can find nowhere else.

In addition to excellent display of grains, grasses, vegetables, canned goods, granite, textiles, ginghams, duck, cotton, and edge tools, commencing with exhibit next to Iowa, at Commissioner's Desk, notice particularly as follows, viz: Model of ship ready for launching, every part of which is made as perfectly as large ship; Bar Harbor row boat, and elegant boat for trout fishing; illustrations of brook trout, of which they sometimes catch, weighing as much as 10 pounds; Indian birch bark canoe; lumberman's accoutrements; wood paper, which is cut from wood; trunk made of leatheroid, a new material manufactured from wood; wood in all conditions necessary for paper-making. One of the finest exhibits of the Exposition is the display of "mohair plush" goods, made by Goodall Manufacturing Co. and Sandford Mills, of robes, table scarfs, upholstery goods, &c., which should have the closest attention of all lovers of the beautiful, and black gros-grain silk in case. Leaving this state, which completes the right wing, pass through Patent Office exhibit, without viewing, to main aisle, down to large globe in U. S. State Department, cross the aisle, and enter Texas exhibit in left wing to the left of large globe, and continue on to the Women's Pavilion.

TEXAS.

Though this state has never before taken part in a World's Exposition, she is certainly making up this time for any former neglect, for, with an enormous space of 18,000 feet on Main Floor, she is displaying a most interesting exhibit. It shows 150 distinct varieties of trees, 360 varieties of grasses, iron, copper, coal, granite, marble, corn, wheat, oats, barley, cotton, wool, sugar, rice, and tobacco; samples from cotton and woolen mills; taxidermy exhibits; an entomological exhibit, comprising 40,000 specimens in glass cases; 21,000 botanical specimens. In center is pagoda, which is dressed with corn, wheat, and cotton, which are the leading products of the state, on eight panels, just beneath the roof, notice statistics, showing area, population, &c., and cotton production, which is 146,785 bales; cereal production, 77,211,485 bushels; live stock, 13,000,000 head; Public School Fund. $80,000,000; State Tax, 20 cents on $100—Assessed Valuation, $1,045,317,136 Number of Schools, 5,236. See, near this pagoda, a large panel giving comparative size of state; near this, and towards front, is the ladies' pavilion, which displays contributions from the ladies of 30 counties in the state, and is very attractive, and well worth careful examination. Notice particularly here, as follows, viz: Screen, painted on matting, by Miss Mary S. Keller, of Dallas: " Una, entering the Witch's Hut," valued at $1,000; at rear of pavilion, wonderful mantel of fossiliferous limestone, in which can be seen many varieties of insects, &c. ; it is ornamented with hand-painted tiles, decorated with the native birds and flowers, the work of several state ladies, doing them great credit; just above mantel is a painting by Mrs. Senator Lamar. Near the ladies' pavilion are cases containing rare specimens of antiquity, minerals, petrifactions, &c.

Notice particularly, as follows, viz: Indian relic on top of case, supposed to be 7,000 years old, belonging to the Mazi people, who existed in Central America prior to the Aztecs. The state geologist, Dr. De Ryee, of Corpus Christi, is a profound scholar in this branch of ethnology, and will give valuable information regarding these peoples.

See portrait of Frederick Schiller, drawn by his sister; old books, in same case; also porcelain figures representing the "five senses," which belonged to the Empress Josephine; decorated plate, which belonged to Prince Eugene, who defeated the Turks. See specimens of gold, onyx, (immense,) beautiful crystal of fluor spar, rose quartz, chloride of silver, excellent mica, baculite petrifactions, table of petrifactions, and wonderful relics dug up at Corpus Christi, specimen of zinc ore, as pure asphaltum as there is in the world. Notice the two-room house made of curly pine, finished without nail or screw, used as office of Commission; also wonderful table, displaying all of Texas woods in mosaic work, and upon this table a water bucket, made of 2 340 pieces of Texas timber. At lower end or front of space is the joint exhibit of the Mo. and Tex. P. R. R., consisting principally of fruits and grains of state. Next, pass from this exhibit into Louisiana.

LOUISIANA.

The exhibit of this state is not only varied and extensive, but of very great interest, especially to persons from the north and west, as the cotton, rice, and sugar culture is so well illustrated. Commencing with the department next to wall, notice particularly, as follows, viz: Specimens of fruits and flowers, both in their natural growth and wax representations; vegetable pear, which is cooked as other vegetables; Okra plant, of which Gumbo is made, and used for cooking; house, made by little girl 12 years of age; magnolia blossom;

new species of sunflower, propagated in New Orleans; wild persimmons, of which beer is made; fruit dipped in rosin—new method of preservation; two kinds of silk cocoons—the white shows that the worms were fed on osage orange leaves, the yellow, that they were fed on mulberry leaves. From the cocoons butterflies are hatched, the butterflies lay the eggs, as you see represented; these eggs hatch silk-worms, which, after they attain their growth, spin the cocoon of silk, and when the cocoons are used for silk, unwound, the worms are not permitted to change to butterflies again—see samples of raw silk; passing back, see specimens of jute and bearded rice; the celebrated Perique tobacco, how put up, &c., raised in no other place in the world but St. James Parish; cotton displayed in all forms, raw and manufactured; next see obelisk showing mechanical products and comparative production of sugar in Louisiana, with other countries; general statistics; see immense cotton plant as it appears in the field in November—it is genuine; next see sugar exhibits—the best sugars and blackest molasses are made by the new centrifugal method, and in this way all the molasses is taken out of the sugar—the lighter-colored syrups were made by the old open-kettle method. Any person wishing to see the manufacture of sugar can do so by visiting ex-Governor Warmouth's plantation just below New Orleans. Governor Warmouth extends invitations to all, and boats run to the plantation; see samples of sugarcane, the ribbon and green varieties; next see specimens of upland and lowland rice in straw, then as threshed—after being threshed, it is taken to the miller and put through a process, hulling and grinding it, obtaining bran, rice-flour, and then rice itself—see specimens of each—the flour and polish are used for food, the bran is fed to stock—see garden showing growth of rice, and obelisk made of rice, showing increase of rice production; specimens of Spanish moss and its preparation for commerce, collars made from it which are not injurious to horses; specimen of Cassa bean, (look some like large cucumber,) used for preserves and pickling; tea plant, see card of explanation; next cotton-seed and its various products; near this, don't fail to see, in case, "The aged couple and their pets," made of cotton, by Mr. Roberts, of New Orleans; wild cane, 30 feet in height, used for fishing-poles and baskets; on case, a jar of peas which are grown to use vines as a fertilizer, said to be excellent; wonderful display of native woods, in bark and in dressed lumber, 150 varieties—cypress, 5½ feet in diameter, yellow ash, red maple, curly pine, finished beautifully; table of native nuts, including pecans, which grow wild in great abundance; black gumwood dressed, similar to mahogany; see little model of house containing 149 varieties of native woods—examine it; column of rock salt, a representation of an inexhaustible supply found in New Iberia Parish; it is very pure; notice an aligator 14 feet long; native ores and minerals, near which is wonderful petrified hickory tree, and a barrel of pork petrified in the river; photograph of remarkable twin tree; views of sugar plantations, illustrating method of manufacture; specimens from sulphur mine, the bed of which is 112 feet thick; collections of birds, among which notice "rice bird," and near these, Indian corn-mill. Leaving this state, next take up Mississippi.

MISSISSIPPI.

The exhibits of this state are deserving of and will repay a careful examination. Commencing at side of building, notice particularly as follows, viz: Wonderful display of canned fruits; immense peaches, and Japanese persimmons, pears, figs, &c., show the state to be remarkable for fruit-growing; second crop of Irish potatoes, planted in August; jutes, grasses, and cotton 11 feet high, remarkable petrifactions, among them the Zenglodon celordes 73 feet long; specimens of native nuts; excellent display of timber, including a cyprus 6 feet in diameter, enormous section of sassafras and hickory; display of fish, including the blanket fish, (spotted;) the flounder, (peculiar shape;) in jar the floater and balloon fish; the stingare, 75 pounds in weight, and is a great enemy of man. Be sure to see "The Burial of Cock-robin" at lower end of exhibits, valued at $750. Interesting exhibits are made by state mills; the wine and silk interests are large; display of silica and glass; specimens of modeling pottery and artistic coloring by Miss Maude Kingsbury; specimens of the tea-plant and dried tea. Next enter

TENNESSEE.

This state may well be proud of its exhibit, for it does it great credit, and is the admiration of all visitors. Commencing at side of building, you see Davidson Co., or Middle Tennessee, exhibit, in which are Early Rose potatoes, the second growth this year asparagus, and sweet potatoes; next to right Shelby Co. exhibit of excellent silk, cotton, and corn; next to right Madison Co. exhibit of enormous sweet potatoes, dried fruits, and cotton; next Robinson Co. exhibit excellent tobacco and millet; next Giles Co. exhibit, made by Mrs. O. M. Spofford; cases at right showing native grasses. You now come to 115 varieties of the famous Tennessee marble, used so generally for furniture. Notice the pure white and deep, rich chocolate; also, the variety known as the landscape marble, white and red, which, when separate, are considered the finest; celebrated ocoëe granite; samples of corn, result of competition for $150 premium; General Jackson's sick chair, and furniture made from the Hermitage. In center column of native woods; case and pyramid of native seeds; next native timber, enormous knot of black walnut, claimed to be worth $1,000; iron and coal; golden eagle, Thos. A. Hendricks.

KENTUCKY.

This state has added a new feature to its exhibit by a display of pictures showing the picturesque, fertile, and striking localities of the state. These comprise 625 transparencies, 60 water-color sketches, and 1,100 card photographs, and should be carefully viewed; in rear next to wall, beautiful collection of preserved fruits and vegetables, by a new process, and vastly important to housekeepers; next, fine collection of timber, comprising white oak and ash, beach, white and yellow poplar; 65 varieties of timber from one county, (Henderson;) coal exhibit, including fine cannel, from undeveloped portion of state, one vein 9 feet 7 inches, and another 7 feet 9 inches; excellent fire-clay, (abundant;) specimens of grasses and grains; specimens of soil from each county; display of iron-ores and building stone; fine display of tobacco and hemp. Next enter Alabama.

ALABAMA.

The exhibit is largely that of the Louisville and Nashville R. R. The state is represented by Prof. Charles Mohr, of Mobile. Commencing with exhibit at end next to center, you find the mineral display, mostly from Birmingham District; notice particularly specimens of coal weighing 10 tons; specimens of two fossil trees, one lying in sections alongside the pile of coal, the other back of large specimen of coal; in these, knots are visible. Iron ore, very rich and excellent, weighing from 5 to 7 tons. Farther on grains and grasses, 180 varieties. See Guinea grass cut 3 times a season; near this Chinese Sugar-cane; just back, cotton-seed cake used for feeding; in bag near it, meal used for fertilizing; to left, towards Missouri, see creosoted wood. Farther along, specimens of fine timber, among which are white ash, yellow poplar, white oak, chestnut, black walnut, wild cherry, cypress, longleaf, or hard yellow pine, curly pine. Octagon pavilion made of Alabama woods and another of Southern pine. Near this, section of immense cypress. Building stone, among which should be noticed fine-grained limestone, finished building stones, crystallized limestone; other valuable stones and fire-clays. Very fine kaolin, or porcelain, earth used for highest grade of porcelain, (No. 48,) asbestus, corundum, (No. 52.)

MISSOURI.

In alcove next to wall is the art department, containing some fine specimens from the Art Museum of St. Louis, also fine exhibit of birds. To left, work of Hydraulic Press Brick Co., of St. Louis; notice fine work in fire-place. Work of inmates of State Blind Asylum. Next to art display is work from Convent of Blessed Sisters, at St. Louis. Farther on, towards front, is pagoda of grains, largely from their Agricultural College. Farther on towards front, the Women's Department, consisting of antiquities, fancy-work, &c.; it makes a good exhibit of minerals, timbers, grasses, cotton, and manufactured articles. Leaving this state, pass on to Arkansas.

ARKANSAS.

This state has great variety of climate and soil, and its immense exhibit includes all the grains and every textile fiber produced by all the other states. Its resources are very great, and as their development is in its infancy, a careful examination of its exhibits will be of interest to the viewer and the state. Notice particularly 137 varieties of timber, 75 of which are commercial woods, specimen of white oak, best in the world, cypress, ash, black walnut, yellow pine, gum tree, and method of preparing last-named, so that it will not warp. Section of huckleberry bush, 12 inches in diameter. Sections of immense grape vine, sumach, elderberry, sassafras, hickory, and oak. Case of commercial woods. Desk of 30 varieties of native woods. Its grasses, with Japan and California clover, and clover 7 feet high; 150 varieties of native grasses; sugarcane, corn, and cotton; iron ores, both hematite and magnetic; wares made of clay; Arkansas honestone; gypsum and wonderful block of quartz; cases displaying large quantities of quartz crystals. Before leaving the state, be sure to visit Mr. J. M. Blake, and see his method of manufacturing Arkansas diamonds; large and interesting display. Pass towards center and enter Georgia.

GEORGIA.

Though this state occupies but a small place in this Exposition, it is well-filled, and its exhibit will be of great interest to visitors, as it displays naval stores and the process of manufacturing turpentine and rosin, which is a novel feature to many. As you enter the exhibit from Arkansas, you find the still with which the turpentine is distilled, and here also you will see the process of manufacture; sections of pine tree showing the cut made necessary to collect the resin, which is distilled, and turpentine and rosin made from it; the rosin is the residuum left after the turpentine is made; you will see different grades of this rosin; see cases showing the manufacture of cotton in all forms, from the cotton-mills in different parts of the State; native woods put up very prettily in book form; model of old steamship "Savannah," the first steamer which crossed the ocean; also model of the new "Savannah," now on line to Europe; old Indian relics; its minerals and metals are beautifully displayed in cases, and are worthy of attention. Leaving this state cross the aisle and view the Queen and Crescent R. R. exhibit, and then passing its pagoda, see the private mineral collection of Mr. A. Foote, of Philadelphia, Pa.

Queen and Crescent R. R., or the Erlenger Syndicate.

This exhibit is collected from eight states, through which it controls roads. It has a large display of minerals and woods, besides many other objects of interest. Notice particularly as follows, viz: In La. ex. a pitch pine grown into an oak; in Miss. ex., remarkable fire-clay; in Ala. ex., iron as melted in the earth; excellent iron ore 73%; red hematite used for paint; piece of brown iron, weighing 10,000 pounds, 93 % iron, from near Birmingham, Ala.; beautiful ferns in fire-clay; cases of china made from Alabama clay (Kaolin): in Tenn. ex., coal from seven different mines, coal and iron display; in Ky. ex., tobacco in all its forms. The locomotive to be here was built by this company from materials obtained along its route, intended to bring President Arthur to this Exposition.

Private Mineral Collection of A. Foote, Esq.

This collection weighs 26 tons, and contains many very interesting specimens. Notice particularly large smoky quartz, from Pike's Peak, fine fold-spar from same place; large quartz in rock crystal; beautiful amethysts; remarkable stalactites of chalcedony; tree trunks of agate lined with amethysts, from Yellow Stone Park; large crystals of beryl; geological map showing the different strata forming the earth's surface.

MARYLAND.

The colors of this state, black and yellow, taken from its coat-of-arms, are very conspicuous. The center of exhibit has the model Battle Monument of Baltimore, around which are cases containing models of birds of state, more than 1,200 specimens. Notice particularly the piano of Charles Carroll, manufactured in London 1789; piano and state council table of Lord Baltimore, which are in Commissioner's office, adjoining; an old vesper bell, brought to America by early Pilgrims, in 1682; old bomb-shell fired by British in attack on Fort McHenry, 1814; the wonderful Entomological collection in cases, finest in this country. The Baltimore and Ohio exhibit, in rear of state exhibit; models of first locomotive run in America, the "Cooper," built and run by Peter Cooper in 1830; second engine, the "Grasshopper;" models of sail car, tread-mill car, and the first passenger car ever used in America; section of first railroad track laid in America; model of original Morse Telegraph and section of wire, and model of plow used in laying it under ground; alongside of this is the new "Selden Sextuplex Telegraph," the latest improvement; also, original of first message ever sent, which was by Mrs. Madison, in 1840; see electric engine of 1851; observe, in glass cases, near Models, report of conductor in 1831, the first coupon ticket, books, &c., pertaining to early days of B. & O. R. R.; photographs of fine scenery along B. & O. road in elegantly furnished alcove of B. & O. R. R. Pass from this state into Delaware.

DELAWARE.

Though this is a small state and has a small space here, it is well filled and tastefully arranged. The display consists largely in manufactured articles, in iron, steel, wood, clay, and gutta-percha. Commencing at wall adjoining Pennsylvania, notice particularly samples of manufactured work of Diamond, Steel and Iron Co. Next, the production of Cusho Machine Co. in case, where see specimens of cold bent iron and steel. Fancy wood work by C. H. Treat & Co., which is made of two or three thicknesses of wood. Also, enameled wood, for placques, &c. Notice display of canned goods; specimens from Vulcanized Fire Co. cotton cans, made of vulcanized rubber, notice how light in weight; knitting machine; case of birds; case of minerals from Delaware College; model of vessel, silver plated, which cost $3,000, one of the most beautiful of the exhibits; models of wooden vessel; ornamental brick and terra-cotta work, illustrated in brick front, representing house 16 feet high. Next you come to Pennsylvania.

PENNSYLVANIA.

The alcove is used mainly for display of manufactured goods and oil paintings of governors. In cases see relics of old linen, read cards, photographs of

U. S. Indian School and students at Carlisle, Pa. This school is the great peace-maker between the whites and Indians. In case of fine shoes, notice light-colored pair, worth $25. In this alcove also are interesting views, illustrating the state manufacture; display of native minerals, grains, and fruits. See display in open frame work, by Robt. Hare, Powell & Co., of Philadelphia, their manufactures, made from their own material; examine carefully. Near this, see huge block of anthracite coal, weighing 3,255 pounds. The lettering is on carved coal. Wonderful display of copper work; display of Reading Coal and Iron Co.; case of relics from battle-field at Gettysburg; glass display from Pittsburgh. Notice name of state, Pennsylvania, made of flowers. From this state enter New Jersey.

NEW JERSEY.

This state has a large and interesting display. Notice particularly as follows, viz: Its fine exhibit of fossils, among which are tooth of Mastodon and oyster shell; case of minerals—see lodestone, zinc ores, and asbestus; excellent clays, and crockery, and terra-cotta, all worthy of careful examination. Examine specimens of green sands, which are used as fertilizers, glass sands, woods, &c.; wampum manufacture, read card of explanation; 12 varieties of cranberries; fine collection of wine from lowlands; Yorktown Centennial vase; improved ice casket. Read table of the state's leading industries on the wall overhead. Next, New York.

NEW YORK.

This state unites its school display with the state exhibit, and commencing in alcove you see first, illustrations of school and college buildings; second, art work of schools, including drawing and original designs; third, charts giving complete statistics of public schools. Next see cabinets showing mineral resources; so far as practicable, the state has shown the resources and their practical use, and for this purpose it displays iron ores, iron, clays, and brick, tile, terra-cotta, marble, monument of building stone 15 feet high. Notice particularly fine photographs and oil paintings among school exhibits in alcove; fine American-Scotch granite, much superior to the foreign Scotch granite, as shown by comparison with samples of each. This collection of stone shows the varieties used in the state capitol at Albany; beautiful and unique ophite-spotted marble of Lake Champlain district. In center is an art building, beautifully decorated, containing excellent display. Next take up West Virginia.

WEST VIRGINIA.

This state displays principally its coal, iron ore, and timber, of which it possesses a great abundance. The variety of its coal display is unequaled at the Exposition, and is extremely interesting. It includes bituminous, semi-bituminous, anthracite, cannel, peacock, and splint coal; it exhibits coal from a 14-foot vein. Notice among this exhibit the celebrated splint coal, which resembles and is nearly as hard as the anthracite, and burns easily without clinkers; beautiful peacock coal, in which may be seen all the colors visible in a peacock feather. This coloring is caused by iron with which it comes in contact. Notice also fine wool display in fleece, and samples, with photographs of sheep from which taken; in exhibit of woods, sections of hemlock from trees growing from 90 to 100 feet without a limb. The state makes a good display of terra-cotta, fire-brick, &c., &c.

VIRGINIA.

Entering this state at the end nearest center, you reach a series of five tables containing minerals from different portions of the state. The first, (yellow,) contains minerals from the Appalachian Chain; the second, (green,) from Shenandoah Valley; upon this case see stalactites from Weyer's Cave; the third, (blue,) from Piedmont Region; the fourth, (purple,) from the midland portion of state; the fifth, (red,) from the tide-waters of Virginia. The woods displayed in crude and polished form, with foliage and in books, are the work of boys of Miller Manual School at Lynchburg. See, also, chess-board of marbleized slate. Near this, granite monuments, by Richmond Granite Co.; Indian relics, including a burr-stone used by Indians for grinding. Back are native minerals, including coal, coke, cannel coal (excellent), manganese, slate, iron ores, hematite, specular and magnetic; lithographic stone, fire-clay, marble, and fossil ores. Next back, native woods, including fine-dressed lumber; next back, display of cotton, tobacco, peanuts, vegetables, grains, fertilizers, &c. Notice particularly the art collection of state, and the model of Natural Bridge, (Va.)

NORTH CAROLINA.

As you enter this exhibit nearest wall, you find the minerals, which extend far down on each side of space, showing gold, silver, copper, iron, mica, and manganese. Gold, silver, and copper ores are from different counties all over the state. Notice particularly as follows: A column and pyramid of phosphates used as fertilizers; cases of mica, and pagoda covered with mica; wonderful leopardite marble, with leopard carved from it; tin ore. Near center, collection of the Hidden gems and diamonds, found only in Alexander Co., and named after Prof. Hidden; nuggets of native gold, worth $2,000; pagoda containing all the grains; excellent canned fruits; botanical and forestry collection, showing the long-leaf pine, tar, turpentine, and pitch industry; table made of 40 kinds of work; pavilion made of dressed woods, very beautifully polished; section of petrified tree; fishery exhibit. Notice here new method of preserving fish to retain natural appearance; and among peculiar fish, the sheephead, porcupine, and sail fish, whose dorsal fins or sails can be shut down at will. It is of sword-fish family, and can kill a shark or whale. The Jew fish on panel high on post; enormous black bass, weighing 50 pounds; also the butterfly toad; great variety of tobacco; huge trunk of Cypress tree 42 feet in circumference.

SOUTH CAROLINA.

Commence at end of exhibit nearest center, where you find the agricultural and horticultural display in the pavilion. Next, see the monument of phosphates. The dark rocks are found in the rivers and the light rocks in the land. Around it are cases of fossils, taken out in mining phosphates, and two sections of earth, showing how the phosphates are found. The large pieces are phosphates taken out of the rivers. There are different brands in jars. See method of manufacture, illustrated. Notice statistical figures on pagoda, made of phosphates, showing over 400,000 tons mined last year, valued at $2,500,000; choice Indian relics and curiosities. Next, fishes, birds, and animals. To left of birds, geology, in which see fossil, hickory, fine kaolin, and in case by fish, imitations of gold bars, showing gold taken from one county last year. Also, beautiful transparent quartz. Next, manufactures including cotton manufacture.

FLORIDA.

Entering this space nearest wall, you first see woods of northern Florida, but to have a proper understanding of them, commence with end next to house in center with magnolia, keeping to right as you pass around and read label on each. Many of these woods are peculiar to this state alone, and, upon careful examination, will be found very interesting. Near these, you will find Indian Fig or rubber tree. Read card on it. In the collection, notice the Florida yew tree and savin or stinking cedar, which are found in no other state. To left below are botanical plants. Above these 45 varieties of native ferns, 30 of which are found only in this state. Under these, woods and barks used for medicinal purposes and coloring. On other side of woods, fruits of northern Florida. Next you come to octagon pavilion, belonging to University of Fine Arts, of Lake de Funiac, which is the Chautauqua of the south, containing works of art, painting, and embroidery. This is a fine display, and should be examined. Beyond this is collection of woods from southern Florida; also, tropical plants. The second table to left is from eastern Florida. Jamaica root, cassava, of which tapioca is made, arrow root. On other side, fruits from eastern Florida, among which are the navy orange, shaddocks, &c. Just here a relief map, which shows counties, principal towns, railroad, and topography of state. Alligator, whalebone, pawpaw, with fruit. Near, branch of cocoa, with fruit. Farther along the pineapple, with fruit. The suckers at base of fruit are used for planting. Next, table of coral and Florida reef plants. In case near octagon is the tortoise turtle and articles made from it. Next on table wooden bowls made from tree; flying and angel fish; ribs of manitee, or sea cow; ancient Latin Bible in black letter.

Center or General Government.

This division of the U. S. Building, commencing at main or street entrance, should be examined by beginning with: 1st. The Smithsonian Institute exhibit, which extends on left to Philadelphia Truss Co.; 2d. Interior Department, commencing with the Geological and Ethnological exhibits, and continuing on right with Railroad Commission, Land Office, and Patent Office display, and Agricultural Exhibit; 3d. Treasury Department on right, including Bureau of Engraving and Printing, and U.S. Light-House Establishment; 4th. War Department on left; 5th. Navy Department on right, including Greely Relief Relics; 6th. State Department, and Post-Office on left.

Smithsonian.

The exhibit of this Institute extends on left from Main Entrance to the exhibit of Philadelphia Truss Co., and is divided as follows, viz: 1st. Archæology; 2d. Ethnology; 3d. Vessel Building and Textiles; 4th. Art; 5th. Smithsonian Exhibits and Fish Commission; 6th. Animal Products and Animal Capture; 7th. Natural History: Birds, Mammals, Shells, and Reptiles; 8th. American Taxidermist Display; 9th. Building Stone and Marble; 10th. Mineralogy and Metallurgy. Notice particularly: 2 scalps, very ingeniously constructed pipes, shields, war clubs, boomerangs, &c., among Indian Relics; an equipped whale-boat; painting in rear entitled "Capturing a Whale." This picture is in Fish Com. Gun for shooting the fin-back whale, which is so gamey as to make it almost impossible to capture with old harpoon method. The harpoons are shot into the whale loaded, and explode in it, thus doubly wounding, and usually killing the monster. Notice, also, brocade cotton, China, Japan, Siam, and Portugese cottons and silks among manufactured cloths. In Art Division see autotypes (a kind of photograph) of all important works of old masters. In Animal Products and mammals, see pair of boots made of a man's skin. In Mineralogy, see cabinet of minerals and a complete collection of gem-bearing rocks of North America, and gems taken from them. Do not fail to give this collection close examination, for here are represented the largest and most valuable diamonds in the world by exact copies, and also a large number of genuine valuable gems; models showing the various methods of smelting.

Geology and Ethnology.

This exhibit of the Interior Department is first at right, viewing General Government Exhibit; It shows mountain formation or growth and the surveys and drawings pertaining to Pueblo Indians and Cliff Builders. Pueblo means village or town, and Pueblo people, or Indians, are those who build and live in towns; the Zuni and Moki are only tribes of Pueblo Indians. This exhibit contains eight models of the dwellings of these Indians of New Mexico and Arizona, which are interesting examples of the highest culture and type of architectural knowledge yet found, pertaining to the early people inhabiting these Western states, and are possibly the connecting link between the high state of civilization shown in architectural remains of Mexico and Yucatan and the wild nomandic tribes of the north. The collections of models of Cliff dwellings further illustrates this connection, if connection there be. These ruins, and the pottery obtained from them, are the only re mains of a tribe which once inhabited all of northern New Mexico, Arizona, and northern Colorado; this display of pottery includes a large collection of this antique pottery, numbering about 200 pieces. The superiority of this pottery over the modern Pueblo ware, which you will find near it, is very readily seen.

U. S. R. R. Commission.

The object of this exhibit is to show the progress of railroad construction west of the Mississippi River from 1860 to 1884, inclusive; also remarkable feats of engineering in that construction, which are illustrated by charts and views. The principal feature of the display is a large chart, 16 feet high and 42 feet wide, executed by hand, which shows the progress of railroad construction west of the Mississippi River from 1860 to 1884, inclusive. This is represented by trains of cars for each year separately, each state or territory taking position in the train according to its relative mileage. On the "way car," at rear of the train, the total mileage is given, and to the right the total mileage of the whole United States is also given. At the end of each decade, elaborate statistics are given, such as number of square miles of territory, to one mile of railroad, population to one mile of railroad, &c.

U. S. Land Office.

This display consists of a series of about seventy-five paintings, illustrating incidents in mining life—both the primitive and present methods—for the purpose of giving the general observer an idea of the manner of procedure in producing the precious and economic minerals of the country. In connection with these are a series of maps, prepared expressly for this Exposition, to show the location of the different mineral deposits, taken from actual developments by practical miners, and not based upon the lines of theoretical geologists. There are also several large cabinets of specimens of ore taken from mines now in successful operation. All of these illustrations are of vast interest, but particular notice should be given to the following, viz: The primitive methods of mining, especially in placer mining, then the improvements made upon it, including the "hydraulic" method, where the water actually washes away hills and mountains. On the other side, you see illustrations of the "pressure box," which is situated on a high elevation, generally many miles distant, and supplies the pipe with water, and produces the great pressure and consequent force. Notice the primitive arrestre, an old Spanish method of mixing the earth containing the gold with quicksilver, beating the combination, making it hard, and then taking it out, they wash away the earth, leaving the precious metals. Salt mining in Cracow, 1,700 feet deep. Here they have mined for 1,200 years, and the timbers displayed are more than 1,000 years old, having been preserved by salt. The illustration of the place where gold was first discovered, Suter's or Marshall's Mill, was made from a sketch taken in 1850. In this exhibit there is also a large and most interesting map, showing comparisons between the "old and new carrying facilities," and the mileage of railroads in the United States on

January 1, 1885. The small locomotive is an illustration of the "Stourbridge Lyon," made from a photograph loaned by John Torrey, Esq., of Honesdale, Pa. It was used for hauling coal cars on a short line of railroad of the Delaware and Hudson River Canal Company, which road was constructed at the head of canal at Honesdale, Pa. It (the engine) weighed 3 tons, was of 9 horse-power, and ran 5 miles an hour. This was the "first locomotive" ever used in the United States, and its first trial trip was from Honesdale to Carbondale, Pa., August 8, 1829. Its boiler was 10½ feet in length, 4 feet in diameter, diameter of wheels 4 feet, and its spokes and felloes were of wood. The crossties of the railroad upon which it ran were 10 feet apart, and not ballasted. The rails were of wood, 12 inches deep, with a strap rail of iron 2½ inches wide and one half an inch thick, fastened on wooden rail by means of screws 4 inches long. The other locomotive on the map represents the "locomotive of to-day," taken from a photograph of an engine built by the Pennsylvania R. R. Its weight is 70,000 pounds, is of 80 horse-power, and its speed 60 miles an hour. A careful view of the map will show the old methods of conveyance—the stage-coach, man going to mill on horseback, &c. See on another map the number of miles of railroad constructed each decade since 1830.

Patent Office.

The object of this exhibit is to show some of the most practical and useful inventions, and improvements upon them. In the center of exhibit is a large painting entitled "The Genius of Invention," in which are the following characters: The large figure is Minerva, the "goddess of invention;" on left, the owl, her chosen bird, representing "wisdom;" under it, the serpent, denoting "subtlety and knowledge;" on right, Jove's Thunderbolts, denoting "electricity;" on right hand of Minerva, stands Vulcan, the blacksmith, balancing a globe on a lever; near him, his blazing forge and ponderous hammer, and at foot, little Mercury with his harp.

Next see photographs of the United States Public Buildings at Washington. D. C., taken by electric light and enlarged; also, a series of photographs showing the progress of invention, which, to be rightly appreciated, should be carefully examined. In viewing display in cases, commence with case nearest Main Entrance and main aisle, which contains electrical machines, and notice, particularly, as follows: Morse's Original Telegraph, Page's Electric Engine; 2d case, Printing Telegraph; 3d case, on upper shelf, Brick and Tile Machines, on lower shelf, Painting and Varnishing Machines, Cloth-Cutting Machines, and Printing and Paper-Folding Machines; 4th case, on upper shelf, Refrigerating and Ice-Making Machines, on lower shelf, Clay and Lime Kilns, Sugar-Manufacturing Machines—1st, old kettle method, 2d, new or centrifugal method—on upper shelf, Soap Machines, and Machines for Cooling Liquids; 5th case, on upper shelf, Apparatus for Signal Service, Machinery for Washing Bottles, &c., on lower shelf, Loaf-Sugar-Making Machinery, Hydraulics, and Chimney-Ventilating Apparatus; 6th case, on lower shelf, Presses, on upper shelf, Hoisting Machinery, and various Mechanical Movements; 7th case, on lower shelf, Tobacco Machinery, on upper shelf, Small Fire-Arms, the original Colt Revolver; 8th case, Large Fire-Arms, notice Needle Gun, in which a needle passes through the powder, and ignites it from the front, thus preventing any portion of the powder from being blown out and retaining full force. Now return to starting-point, and commence second row of cases, so as to get the exhibits in their order. 1st case, Cotton Jennys and Spinning Machines; notice original Eli T. Whitney Jenny; 2d case, Knitting and Weaving Machinery; 3d case, Pulp-Making Machine; 4th case, Machines for making Paper, Envelopes, and Felt Hats; 5th case, Illuminating and Heating Apparatus, and Safety Lamps—notice stove for burning straw, tin water-lamp, for attracting fish, large iron candlestick, on which pine-knots were burned, in early days; 6th case, Invalid beds, bedsteads, cribs; &c.; 7th case, Bedsteads, bed-springs, &c.

Now pass back to front aisle, and along to the first or second row of cases, which contains plows and harrows; second case, seeds, sowers, shovels, planters, &c.; third case, Harvesters, rakes, &c.; fourth case, Hay-cutters and harvesters; fifth case, Agricultural and Mining Machinery; sixth case, Milling machinery; seventh case, Row-locks, screw-propellers, paddle-wheels, steering and propelling machinery, among which see Abraham Lincoln's Boat; eighth case, Life-preserving Apparatus and Tanning Machinery; ninth case, Leather-Working and Boot and Shoe Making Machinery; tenth case, Sewing Machines; see original Howe and First Continuous Thread Machine; eleventh case, Metal-Working Needle Machines and Dairy Machinery; twelfth case, Injectors and Ejectors for Boilers, Power Hammers, and Metal-Working Machinery; thirteenth case, Boiler Furnaces, Grate Bars, and Apparatus for Feeding Fuel and Air Smoke-Stacks and Exhaust Apparatus; fourteenth case, Governors and Steam Hammers, Boiler Furnaces, &c.; fifteenth case, Rotary and Oscillating Engines; sixteenth case, Steam Apparatus; see old Ross Winan's Locomotive, and the old Tompkins Engine, with peculiar short cylinder and long stroke.

Agricultural Department.

The object of this exhibit is to show the practical working of the department in furnishing information to farmers, horticulturists, &c. The exhibit furnishes information by means of valuable maps, plates, charts, &c.; charts showing area of cereal and textile culture, timber lands, farming lands, relative growth of different cereals and textiles in different states, and exports of each. Samples of wools and other textiles and fabrics; samples of cane and sorghum sugar, with analysis of each; specimens of grasses, with their chemical products; native American woods, with their uses and chemical products. The silk culture in various phases; also bee culture, with artificial comb; casts showing various fruits of the U. S.

Entomological display showing insects fatal to growth, and means of destroying them; illustrations of all fungi. Notice particularly as follows, viz: House illustrating silk-worm culture, bee culture, samples of sugar and candy made from sorghum sugar. Among the grasses, notice blue grass of stockmen, bunch and gramma grasses, mountain timothy, tall valley grass.

War Department.

The object of this exhibit is to show the practical workings of the Department in caring for its sick and wounded, on the field and in the hospital, and for this purpose it has divided the exhibit into five classes, viz: 1st, models of hospitals and hospital tents, with descriptions; 2d, medical and hospital supplies, and treatment of sick and wounded soldiers in field and hospital; 3d, means of transportation of sick and wounded on land and water, consisting of ambulances, stretchers, litters, and cacoletes, (chair saddles,) and models of travorps, (horse litters,) U. S. Medical Transport Car, models of hospital cars of the Army of the Cumberland and Potomac; hospital steamers and steamships; St. John's Ambulance Association, litters, stretchers, ambulance, hampers, bandages, and splints; 4th, methods employed for systematic study of diseases, with a view to better treatment of sick and wounded soldiers—to illustrate which the Army Medical Museum is represented by specimens from medical, surgical, and microscopical collections; specimens illustrating normal human anatomy; comparative otology and histology; photographic specimens; surgical instruments and appliances; microscopes, culture apparatus, micro organisms growing in various media, &c.; 5th, miscellaneous, including portraits of eminent U. S. A. Surgeons; large map of U. S. showing locations of different military stations and diseases prevailing at these stations; this map is of vast interest on left side is a "key" that explains it. The exhibits are labeled, and a little care will enable the visitor to understand what he examines.

Engraving and Printing Bureau.

This branch of the Treasury Department exhibits two large frames containing specimens of Government bonds and Treasury notes, of all denominations from $10,000 down; also specimens of internal revenue stamps engraved; vignette portraits of all men prominent in American history or politics, and steel engravings of public buildings at Washington, D. C.

Light-House Board.

This is also a branch of the Treasury Department, and makes its display just back of the Engraving and Printing Bureau.

Notice particularly model of Tower Rocks Light-House; Spectacle Reef, Lake Huron Light-House, and the coffer dam used in building it—the crib is first built, then the coffer dam is placed in it; model of Light Ship on Delaware Bay, with peculiar mushroom anchor, which holds the boat; model of Minot's Ledge Light-House, eight feet high, which cost $6,000; 4th and 5th class lenses are here, the larger of which cost $6,000—the largest could not be brought, but the lamps of every class may be seen; models of Bell Buoys and Whistling Buoys used to guide the mariner; interesting map on wall, showing light-house, and life-saving stations in United States; directly back of light-house display, see exhibit of United States Coast and Geodetic Survey, with large and small instruments used in the surveys, together with government standards of measure; model showing land elevations of United States and depths of the Gulf of Mexico, and the Bay of North America, (Atlantic Ocean), notice at lower right-hand corner, the great depth of Bay of North America, which is over five miles.

State Department.

The object of this display is to exhibit the industries of various nations of the world. Notice particularly as follows, viz: The interior of large globe, which is decorated with bandwork of every nation, is 50 feet in diameter, in center, chandelier from Japan; on glass, statistical tables of commerce of the world; it is divided into six compartments, representing the six geographical divisions, and in each compartment are articles showing the customs, habits, and industries of the people of that division; also picture illustrations; Egyptian pottery, in Africa section; linens, laces, &c., in Europe; outside o_ globe, full display of cottons manufactured for foreign trade—read labels; furniture and other articles made of teakwood, the hardest wood in the world; illustrations of cattle and sheep industries of the world; ornamental woods, carvings, spices, and mattings from India; screens and drawings illustrating tea industry in China; the ship builder's models, including a "monitor;" illustrations of agricultural interests of Japan, also Japanese bamboo fence.

Navy.

The Greely Relief Exhibit; on table near center different kinds of clothing used in Arctic regions, one suit of underclothing, worth $110; mode of dressing feet—four coverings; knapsack, with contents as stated on card; little model of dog sled, made of ivory, in glass case; two large whale boats, which carried the dead from "The Bear"; ice anchor, ice auger, snow sledges, Canadian toboggan (sled); see pyramid of provisions used in Arctic expedition; at farther end see Esquimaux Hyack, (boat,) and man in it; at end near door are dummies showing dress in Arctic region—notice particularly harness around them; dummy of Esquimaux girl, whose dress looks rather light for the climate, but upon examination you will find the dress is lined with eiderdown, making it sufficiently warm; photographs in center showing progress of Greely Relief Expedition; see their living tent, near end of exhibit. On second platform in Navy, see torpedoes, near corner, which are fired by electricity; electric search lights, which are American patent, but manufactured in France; one of these is generally placed on each side of the bow of a vessel to discern the position of an enemy or approach of a torpedo; the largest of these great concave reflectors is of 60,000 candle power and throws a light from ten to fifteen miles; powder mine, used for sinking in port; row of charges of powder, and cases in which they are carried; case of guns and pistols, including Revolutionary musket and Hotchkiss new repeating rifle; see here, also, sharp pikes, called boarding pikes, used at port-hole to prevent boarding boat; near corner, Dahlgren breech-loading rifle cannon, and at corner, huge revolving five-barrel cannon, American patent, (Hotchkiss,) made in Paris, range 1,000 yards, fires sixty times a minute, fires shell; next, a Gatling gun—

1,300 balls can be fired in a minute; next, a peculiar gun, called Billinghurst; next, table of projectiles—the white are shrapnel shells filled with musket balls, the red are the ordinary shells, the brown are canister; the largest canister weighs 410 pounds, and the entire case is put into gun; see apparatus for working guns aboard ship; next, old Mexican gun, used in Mexican war; next, three old Spanish guns, one, a breech-loader, was made in 1490, and used by Cortez in conquest of Mexico. On third platform, in rear, see ship's galley, (store and kitchen combined)—this is not so large as the generality of them; back of this, see immense torpedo—carbonic acid gas is the propelling power, and the whole is controlled by electricity; see crematory, and read card of explanation; line of port-hole models, from 1 to 4, intended to show improvements in ventilation.

Life-Saving Buoy, see card of explanation; section of boat showing sick-room on board vessel, called "Sick Bay;" two models of rifle guns, same size as originals—the largest is as follows: weight, 54,000 pounds, charge of powder, 250 pounds, projectile, 500 pounds, velocity, 2,000 feet per second, penetration, 22-inch wrought-iron plate, range 11 miles—it is a 10-inch gun to be used on monitors; the smaller, weight, 27,000 pounds, charge of powder, 125 pounds, projectile, 250 pounds, velocity, 2,000 feet per second, penetration, 7-inch wrought-iron plate, range 9 miles, to be used on new cruisers Chicago and Atlanta, the models of which are here. Next, to left, is Post-Office, around and above which, together with the State and Navy Exhibits, is a miniature "electric railway." This completes the exhibits on main floor of this building. Now, ascend the left-hand stairway, and commence with the "New England" exhibit of the Women's Department, and proceed on towards the Educational Department.

WOMEN'S ASSOCIATION DEPARTMENT.

This department occupies the west gallery, adjoining educational department on one side and the colored people's department on the other side. Their object is to illustrate the educational, artistic, industrial, and inventive work of women; the states are divided into groups, namely: 1st, to right, North-western states, comprising Illinois, Indiana, Iowa, Michigan, Minnesota, Nebraska, Dakota Territory, Montana Territory, Wyoming Territory, Wisconsin, Colorado; 2d, South-western states, comprising Kentucky, Missouri, Arkansas, Tennessee; 3d, Southern states, comprising Florida, Alabama; 4th, Middle states, comprising New York, Pennsylvania, New Jersey, Delaware; 5th, New England states, displaying their exhibits as one group. In addition there is the Scientific and Literary Society, situated back of the South-western group; National Women's Temperance Union, situated at head of the stairs; next to this, the Creole exhibit; next, Christian Women's Exchange, located in Alcove; also, Art Gallery, displaying French flowers.

NEW ENGLAND STATES. This exhibit displays industrial-art scientific work by women; photographs and reports of schools for women, among which is Wellesley College, which has an excellent reputation and is delightfully situated.

NEW JERSEY.—Notice particularly dress worn by Mrs. Ermina Smith, the Commissioner, when she was baptized after her adoption by the Iriquois Indian chief; it is made of blue broadcloth, embroidered with white wampum and silver buckles. In same case is a papoose's cradle with Indian doll, and a war-rattle made of turtle-shell, Indian banner illustrative of buffalo hunt, pottery and bead work by Indian women, samples of linen plucked, hackeled, spun, woven, and bleached by Early Dutch Settlers. In Art, see painting, "New Mown Hay;" placque painted by Miss Nelson, etching in case, log-cabin quilt, silk display, and photograph of bas-relief of "Mollie Pitcher," the heroine of New Jersey.

MISSISSIPPI.—Notice particularly large case of crazy work, including one piece of very fine mosaic, hair wreath said to contain hair of Washington and many of his successors; the lady spent two years in making it; painting representing corn and cotton, wreath made of scales of silver fish, rag carpet made by a lady 77 years old, and is really beautiful, examine; beautiful lambrequin in case, a charcoal drawing entitled, "The Tribute to the Minotaur;" pink satin reticule 104 years old, table cloth 400 years old.

KENTUCKY. The ladies of this state have made a wonderful display of the antique. See old work done by ladies, while others stood on watch for Indians; flax work in every phase, with old flax spinning-wheel; portraits of General Jackson and Daniel Boone; a Boston, Mass., Gazette of 1774, in case on wall; handkerchief that ran the blockade, a crayon by the Elder Peel, a poker sketch, carved mahogany chairs, case from the Ladies' School of Pharmacy at Louisville. Leaving this portion of the Women's Department, enter the Educational Department, and commence with the exhibit from Bath, England.

EDUCATIONAL DEPARTMENT.

Leaving the Women's Department and passing along the gallery, you come to the Educational Department, one of the best and most instructive exhibits in the Exposition, and should be carefully examined by all visitors. Commencing at corner of gallery, the various exhibits of cities, schools, societies, and states are as follows, and in following order, viz: 1st. Bath, England; 2d. Kindergarten and Kitchen Garden; 3d. France; 4th. U. S. Bureau of Education; 5th. Industrial branch of High School of Tulane University, with an annex exhibit of wood work from Swedish Schools; 6th. Miscellaneous exhibit of industrial work by Special Schools; 7th. Christian Brothers; 8th. Ward's Natural History; 9th. New Hampshire; 10th. Wilkes-Barre, Pa.; 11th. Iowa; 12th. Minnesota; 13th. Louisiana, including N. O.; 14th. Nebraska; 15th. Indiana; 16th. Ohio; 17th. Florida; 18th. Tennessee; 19th. Virginia; 20th. School exhibit; 21st. Missionary Societies, particularly those engaged with Colored People and Indians.

BATH, ENGLAND.—Here you will see models of ancient Roman baths, during the period that Rome governed England, in contrast with the modern baths of that city, together with illustrations of fine natural scenery surrounding the city.

KINDERGARTEN SCHOOL. This exhibit is in charge of Mrs. A. B. Ogden; its object is to illustrate that method of teaching. It is absolutely necessary, for the proper conduct of the school, for persons desiring to see the teaching to make private application to Mrs. Ogden, after school hours, when arrangements will be made.

FRENCH EXHIBIT.—This exhibit is organized under the auspices of Public Instruction and Fine Arts. It is shown in nine rooms or divisions, illustrating, respectively, by plans, &c., the progress made in France in School Architecture and Decoration, and methods of teaching. It bears especially upon the primary, higher primary, professional, apprenticeship, and art schools, and Normal Colleges. In the first rooms, the visitors should notice the models of a creche, exhibited by the Societi des Crèches; a set of six plans on school architecture, as types of improved cheap schools recently erected in France; also, the panels for decoration of school-rooms; a set of cheap prints and casts, to form a type of art museum for elementary schools, in order to initiate, as far as possible, every child to a sense of the beautiful; also, a collection of reward cards for the same purpose. On table extending along window side, are, chiefly, works of infant and primary schools; in center of rooms are specimens of manual work by boys and girls of Elementary and Professional schools; near balustrade, selected specimens of school furniture, museum and didactic material, geographical and scientific. The center part of the exhibit contains displays from the Primary Schools of Paris; next, plans of Secondary Schools and Universities, and publications for schools of every grade. The last room illustrates drawing and decorative art; notice, specially, collection of casts for drawing models; also, panels of drawings by pupils of various elementary schools and training colleges, and schools of industrial and decorative art; a frame of drawings, executed by candidates at the examination for certificates of drawing-master in public schools.

CHAUTAUQUA.—The object of this exhibit is to explain the plan or method of working and scope of the Chautauqua University. You will be shown that, at a trifling expense and a limited amount of time, you can obtain a thorough collegiate course. All will be explained by Prof. Swing, who is in charge, and who does fine clay modeling for the interest of visitors.

U. S. BUREAU OF EDUCATION.—This exhibit comprises voluntary specimens from throughout the United States, and embraces nearly every phase of teaching, training, education, school architecture, school apparatus, and graded school-books. This display includes such representations in the following order, viz: School architecture; illustrations in primary work; historical exhibit, which includes a model of U. S. Capitol; the Washington, D. C., school exhibits; Normal School of Baltimore, Md.; next, Amherst College exhibits; exhibit of Civil Engineering, from the University of Pennsylvania, with models; exhibit of Chicago public schools. Notice, particularly, mechanical and art drawings; also, wood-carving and pattern-cutting. Back of this is the Gymnasium, in charge of Prof. Hasting Nisson, of Washington, D. C., with apparatus for schools and families, after the Swedish System, which is considered the best. Prof. Nissen gives illustrations at half past ten and half past eleven, A. M., and from one to two and three o'clock, P. M.; next, School of Design for Women, at Philadelphia, Pa.; near here, in cases, next to aisle, are Bibles printed in every language; next, chemical exhibit; next, medical school; next, deaf mutes and blind; next, industrial or reform school; and last, work of the feeble-minded. Next, turning to side aisle, you reach

MECHANICAL BRANCH OF HIGH SCHOOL, TULANE UNIVERSITY.—The object of this exhibit is to show the work done by students in connection with their regular studies. They are not taught a particular trade, but the general principles of all trades. This school is in charge of Prof. Ordway; see the exhibit he has of work of Swedish schools. Next this are displays from various industrial schools in New York and Massachusetts, &c.

CHRISTIAN BROTHERS.—This organization is 200 years old, and the object of this exhibit is to show the works of their normal, parochial, and industrial schools, colleges, and academies, making it very interesting, especially in their methods of teaching, and should be carefully and thoroughly examined by those specially interested in education. Notice, particularly, their method of instruction in their industrial schools—they not only teach a trade, but require the pupil to know every possible fact concerning process, origin, &c., pertaining to it; also, excellent method of teaching, by way of illustrations, geography, geology, and conducting class talks. Brother Noah is in charge of the exhibit, and will very kindly give any information concerning it desired.

WARD'S NATURAL SCIENCE ESTABLISHMENT.—This collection comprises Zoology, Geology, and Mineralogy, and makes a very instructive and interesting display. The mammoth, which first arrests one's attention, is 16 feet high, and 26 feet in length to curve of tusks. The great lizard, 23 feet long, the Irish elk, and many of the large animals whose pictures are on the wall, are not in existence, and belong to pre-historic ages. Notice, particularly, the following: Copy of the famous Rosetta Stone, at end next to Christian Brothers read cards of explanation; near this, casts (actual size) of gold nuggets found; farther along, a septarium (over-case) from Weymouth, England, which is a clay concretion, with calcite interspersed; on end of next case, see immense beryl; on wall, high up, see giant crab of Japan, sword fish, turtles, &c.; on case, large sponge growth, (paterion neptuni); on wall in center, large bird tracts from Connecticut Valley; in last case, next wall, models showing form of crystallization of minerals and metals; also, casts of gold nuggets and imitation of precious and principal gems.

NEW HAMPSHIRE.—This exhibit contains charts showing general school system; work in penciling and drawing; specimens of kindergarten work; map-drawing, penmanship, &c.

WILKES-BARRE, PA.—This exhibit is from Third District Public Schools, and consists of, 1st, bound volumes of examinations; 2d, wall and portfolio work of drawing; 3rd, views, plans, and cost of High School and other schools; 4th, samples of promotion papers, rewards of merit, reports, &c; 5th, vocal music, plan books, &c.

IOWA.—This exhibit demonstrates that Iowa ranks among the first in school system. Some of her methods of instruction are admirable, and deserve careful attention. Its object is to show these methods throughout their entire school system, including the University. Notice, particularly, interesting charts showing school statistics; method of primary instruction; work of university students, comprising mechanical, free hand, and map drawing, and exhaustive treatment of particular subjects in theses—examine bound books containing these theses; specimens of map and mechanical drawing; work of the blind, deaf, and dumb. The exhibit is in charge of Professor T. H. McBride, of the State University, who deems it a pleasure to impart any information concerning their admirable methods of instruction.

MINNESOTA.—The university of this state consists of four colleges and a normal school, and the exhibit is intended to illustrate all. Notice particularly, in Mechanical Arts, manufactured work of students, and their first, second, and third exercises; geometrical drawing and tests of strength of materials. In College of Science and Literature, charts illustrative of instruction; the College of Agriculture and Geological Survey are represented in state exhibit on main floor. In Normal School, drawings, penmanship, kindergarten work, and charts made by student-teachers—good work; charts on walls showing studies taught, and colored maps made by teachers; Howard's Electrical Sidereal Clock. Notice, also, display of St. Paul's eighteen public schools, and work in drawing and crayon sketches; home-made school apparatus, by the Stillwater School, made in school, at odd hours, at a trifling cost.

LOUISIANA, INCLUDING N. O.—This exhibit includes work from the primary schools, specimens of botanical work of the junior class in High School. Notice, particularly, map drawing, penciling, and geometrical drawing.

NEBRASKA.—Here the State Normal School makes an exhibit; also, the private school, "St. Clare Hall," of Miss Clara Link, of Lincoln, of artistic work; see illustrations of school buildings, and tables of school statistics.

INDIANA.—This exhibit includes that of the public schools of Lafayette and LaPorte, illustrating work in clay molding and drawing; also, illustrations of various kinds of work of primary students.

OHIO.—The exhibit of this state shows a fine system of giving statistics, but, as will be seen, they are quite old. The Public Schools of Columbus make a very creditable display.

FLORIDA.—This exhibit shows the work of graded schools of the state. Examine charts showing the plan of studies in the graded and high schools.

TENNESSEE.—This exhibit is made largely by the Vanderbilt University, of which see table of statistics; Tennessee Female College, Ward's Seminary, &c.

VIRGINIA.—The exhibit from this state is from her public schools, and illustrates mechanical and map drawing, and general school work. Notice illustrations of school-buildings.

SCHOOL APPARATUS.—This is an exhibit of microscopes, telescopes, and eye-glasses, &c., made by Rausch & Lamb, of Rochester, N. Y. Opportunity is offered to persons to view objects through these instruments.

AMERICAN MISSIONARY SOCIETIES.—This exhibit shows work from a large number of schools for the Colored People and Indians, of which their entire number is 62 and teachers 280. They are doing a wonderful work, and attention should be given to the exhibit. Leaving this department, pass to the Colored People's Department.

COLORED PEOPLE'S DEPARTMENT.

This exhibit commences at the north-east corner, and occupies the north end. It comprises the respective states and territories, as follows, and in following order, viz: Sec. A, Virginia and West Virginia; Sec. B, Tennessee: Sec. C, Kentucky; Sec. D, North Carolina; Sec. E, Alabama; Sec. F, Mississippi; Sec. G, Louisiana; Sec. H, South Carolina, Florida, and Texas: Sec. I, Georgia and Arkansas; Sec. K, Delaware, District of Columbia, and Maryland; Sec. L, Pennsylvania, Ohio, Indiana, Minnesota, and Kansas; Sec. M, New Jersey; Sec. N, New York; Sec. O, Missouri, Iowa, Illinois. Wisconsin, Michigan, and Nebraska; Sec. P, New England States: Sec. Q, New Mexico, Wyoming, Utah, Idaho, Nevada, and Colorado. These exhibits should be visited by all, for a most creditable display will be found. Nearly every state has one or more inventions by colored people, and the New York Exhibit has a number that are very ingenious and useful, some of which are by boys of fourteen or fifteen years of age. The display of Art Work, in almost every variety, is certainly very commendable, among which those of Washington, D. C., and Louisiana are quite remarkable, and should have special attention. The displays of Kentucky and Alabama are excellent. Even the far-off territories are represented here. New Mexico has a varied collection, including a remarkable collection of old coins, one weighing two pounds, worth but $1. The Commissioner has also mineral cabinets on exhibition, which are for sale. Leaving this department, pass around to the Women's Department, and complete examination of same. As many of these states and territories had not displayed their exhibits when we went to press, they consequently are not described.

NEBRASKA.—Notice Indian women's work; lace work from a convent; banner containing coat-of-arms of each state in the Union—good; copy of "Beatrice," from the original in Rome; "Husked Corn," copy; "Market Girl," "Christmas Tree," "Pelicans;" agricultural wreath, made of seeds—quite a novelty; hand-painted china, and fine display from silk culture.

MINNESOTA.—Notice, particularly, among paintings, "The Upper Mississippi to Lower," "Fort Snelling in 1861," sketch in oil, on glass, of "Falls of Minnehaha;" panel-piece, on easel, "The Italian Sailor's Wife" a placque, "Tell Me," two school-girls, one teasing for the other's secret: "Sleeping Captive," painted from a cast by Michael Angelo; a set of tiles, in mantel forms, representing "Hiawatha's Wooing;" a set of china plates, with lily designs; child's set, decorated. The gem of the display is the autograph quilt, containing autographs of many of the most prominent military and literary men and statesmen in the world of the present age.

IOWA.—It is to be regretted that much of the interesting exhibit of this state was destroyed by railroad accident. Notice zephyr work, illustrated in animals, &c.; modeling in plaster, including casts of Justice Miller and ex-Secretary Harlan; decorated mirror, oil paintings and water-colors, large portrait of a bride, crazy work, and decorated china.

THE MAIN BUILDING---1378x905 feet.

FACTORIES AND MILLS 850x120 FEET.

MACHINERY ANNEX.

INDIANA.—Notice, particularly, a rug of tufted work, lined with red satin; table scarf, embroidered, with three owls in consultation, in brown silk, and edged with chenille balls; feather-work, patented by a lady; this work appears in great variety; a trunk, made by a woman 69 years old; copyright book, showing territorial growth; Columbia ironer, patented; silk exhibit; work in wood and brass; carved cabinet of cherry; several fine paintings, by Miss Cora Campbell; portrait of Bishop Talbot; a painting, "Threading Needle for Margy."

WOMEN'S EXCHANGE.—This organization takes the work of women, and disposes of it for them on commission, and its profits are used for charitable purposes, and for this reason they only are permitted to sell goods. The exhibit is very fine, being made up of nearly every kind of women's work. Notice, particularly, needle-work on satin, representing the cotton plant in various stages of blossom; vase of flowers, crocheted of silk; rare old laces, made in the fifteenth and sixteenth centuries; silk wedding slippers, worn in 1787.

W. N. T. U.—In this exhibit, the states are all grouped together, and display methods of work and evidences of results gained in individual work.

Here you complete the examination of the U. S. Building, and pass over to the Main Building, entering door at end nearest U. S. Building, and pursue course as Guide directs. On the way over to Main Building, notice Taft's Electric Railway.

The Electric R. R. between the U. S. Building and Main Building receives its electrical motive power from a plant in the Main Building, which is conveyed by wire to the track, and from the track the coach receives the current of electricity, which propels the train along the track.

MAIN BUILDING.

General Description.

Length, 1,378 feet; width, 905 feet; height to gallery, 23 feet; height from gallery floor to rafters, 23 feet; height of front elevation, 60 feet; height of tower, 115 feet; square feet of space, 1,403,840; square feet of gallery floors, 206,000; square feet of offices, 46,460; total square feet, 1,656,300; number of acres, 33; length of Music Hall, 375 feet; width, 164 feet; incandescent electric lights, 15,000; arc lights, 700; total length of all aisles, 6 miles 300 feet. The ends of building front nearly north and south, respectively; the sides nearly east and west, respectively. The north end is that next the U. S. Building. The main entrance is at center of east side, or side to left as you come from U. S. Building. Music hall is nearly in center, directly back from main entrance. The building is occupied with the following exhibits, viz: In center, on each side of Music Hall, are Foreign Exhibits, in following order, on left of Music Hall: 1st. Austria and Hungary. 2d. Italy. 3d. France. 4th. Great Britain and Ireland. 5th. Germany. 6th. Republic of Honduras. Next, back and west of this, Japan. Back and west of this, China. Next, back and west of this, British Honduras. Turning to left, you find Spain. Interspersed among these are representations from other countries, which will be taken up in their order further on. To the right of Music Hall are, 1st, Russia, and 2d, Belgium.

On the front, or east side, back of Music Hall, are Miscellaneous Exhibits, many of which are of great interest, and the Guide indicates where special attention should be given. Back of foreign exhibits, music hall, and agricultural department is Machinery Hall, including the great engines, the cotton and silk manufactures, the cold storage-rooms, refrigerators, and ice manufacturing machines, which are in operation. This department should be visited by both ladies and gentlemen, for nearly everything is of greatest interest and easily accessible, though from a distance it might not appear to be so. There are easy and safe steps on and over the platform upon which great engines rest, and by following Guide, no difficulty will be experienced. Back of machinery is the boiler-house, in which are all the boilers where the steam is generated. Machinery Annex, 120×570 feet, in which will be found a large variety of machinery running and working.

On the north end, or next to the U. S. Building, is Department of Agricultural Implements, which should be visited by both ladies and gentlemen, as it contains the finest machinery in the world, and much that is curious—the Guide indicates when to notice particularly. For convenience of visitors, I have divided the building as follows, viz: 1st, Miscellaneous Exhibits, which lie on the east side, or left, as you enter end towards U. S. Building; 2d, Agricultural Implements, commencing at north or end towards U. S. Building; 3d, those Foreign Exhibits that are north of music hall, or adjoining agricultural exhibit; 4th, Machinery Hall, next to the foreign exhibits, south of music hall; 5th, Miscellaneous Exhibits, on south end which you enter from machinery hall; 6th, Galleries. In Main Tower, there are chimes, which are rung daily by Prof. F. Widdows, of Washington D. C., the celebrated master of this art. In Music Hall, there are, every day, band music, and organ music on grand organ, built by Pilcher Bros., of New Orleans, for this occasion. Over Main Entrance, in front, is an interesting group, comprising, in the foreground, a stately female, pointing westward with wand and leading a huge bison; upon back of bison sits an Indian female; on right is female—"emblem of peace"—on left is another on the war-path. This is a copy of a group in Hyde Park, London, but is peculiarly adapted to America. It was manufactured by Messrs. Bakewell & Co., of Salem, Ohio. Below, in niche on right, is a statue of Columbus: in niche on left, statue of Washington, and below, in center over entrance, Coats-of-Arms of Louisiana and Mississippi.

General Directions for Main Building.

The name of the exhibitor and his exhibit, with letter and number of post where he is located, is given in Guide; so, by consulting the Index to Main Building, any exhibitor and his exhibit can be found. By following the letters and numbers of posts, and directions of Guide as to making turns, the viewer can begin anywhere; but the best way is to commence as Guide directs, at the end and entrance nearest U. S. Building, and take Miscellaneous Exhibits first, and others in the order indicated. Wherever it is thought that the visitor might be interested unusually, the Guide directs special notice. The lettering and numbering commence in the south-west corner, [the letters running from W. to E., the numbering from S. to N.,] with letter A and No. 1;

then the same letter is on the same line of posts the entire length of building, but the numbers increase with posts, as A 1, A 2, &c. Each letter is used twice, for instance, the next post to east of A 1 is AA 1, then B 1 and BB 1, and so on through the alphabet to VV; so, in locating a party, turn to Index, get his letter and number, and you can readily find him. I have thought it best, except when especially directed, for visitors to view the exhibit on one side of the aisle only at a time. It would be well for a person to glance over his Guide previous to viewing exhibits, and mark with pencil that which has special attention called to it, and any that he might think he would care particularly to see, and in this way be sure to see everything of importance. By following Guide, and at the end of a day or any time of viewing, checking the last exhibit viewed, nothing will be overlooked. The visitor must, by all means, examine displays in the Gallery, for some of the finest exhibits are there.

V.V, 61, Ladies' Dressing-Room.
V, 58, A. Kilpstein, Chemicals and Drugs, and Frederick Brown, Prep.Gingers.
V, 57 and 56, Samuel Cabot, Jr., Creosote Wood, Stains, and Lampblack.
V, 56 and 55, Biliousine, Patent Medicine.
V, 56 and 55, Am. Paper Box Co.
V, 55 and 54, Electrine Magic Cleaner.
V, 55 and 54, Egyptian Chemical Co., Embalming Materials.
V, 54 and 53, T. Engelbach, Homœopathic Pharmacists, N. O.
V, 53, Gillam's Sons, Embossed Envelopes.
V, 53 and 52, Hard Rubber Co., Brushes, Combs, &c.
V, 52, Am. Standard Drop Shot Co.
V, 52, Denler's Bitters.
V, 51, Durrie and McCarty, Hardware and Manufacturers' Agents.
V, 49 to 48, Parker & Drigs.
V, 48 and 47, Norton Door Check and Spring.
V, 47 and 46, Hance Brothers and White, Manufacturing Chemists.
V, 45 and 44, E. J. Hart & Co., Crude Drugs and Chemical Preparations.
V, 43, Reed & Co., Chemicals and Medical Preparations.
V, 41 and 40, Excelsior Pottery Works—notice beautiful vases.
V, 39 and 38, Southern Express Co.
V, 37 and 36, Western Union Telegraph.
V, 36 to 33, R. R. Ticket Office, where tickets are stamped for return.
V, 33 to 30, Main Entrance and Aisle, which you cross to
V.V, 27 to 26, Office of Chief of Transportation.
V.V, 25, Office of Director General.
V, 24 to 22, Granite Iron Co.; excellent display; examine.
V, 21 to 19, Lalance and Grosjean Manufacturing Co., Agate Iron Ware, Japanned and Stamped Ware.
V, 17 and 16, Ideal Coffee Pot Manufacturing Co. and Centrifugal Mixer.
V, 16, Marietta Hollow Ware and Enameling Co.
V, 16 and 15, A. & H. Myers, Pure Whiskies.
V, 15, Elizabeth (N. J.) Paraffine Works—Paraffine Goods.
V.V, 14, John King, Glass Goods, and John Evans, Lamp Chimneys.
V, 15, W. H. McBryers, Pure Whiskies.
V, 13, Smith & Anthony & Co., Stoves and Ranges.

V.V, 12, Chief of Installation Office.
V, 12 to 11, Iowa Farming Tool Co.
V, 11 to 10, Black Diamond File Works.
V, 10 to 9, Inman Steamship Line see model steamer—and American Ship Windlass Co.
V, 9 to 8, American Ultra Marine Works, Marine Colors.
V, 8, Hemingray Glass Co.
V, 8 to 7, John W. Fisher, Cooking Crocks.
V, 6 to 5, F. O. Cross, Rustic Monument Works.
Passing under stairs and turning to left, come to Samuel Bent & Co., Iron, Nickle, and Brass Stable Goods.
Turning back to same aisle, you come to U.U, 5 and 6, Manning Co., Ranges.
U.U, 6, St. Louis Wrought-Iron Range Co.; examine.
U.U, 7 to 8, Phœnix Glass Co.; examine.
U and U.U, 9 to 10, Detroit, Mich., Stove Works; examine.
U and U.U, 11, Bridgeford & Co., Stove and Ranges; examine.
U and U.U, 14 and 16, Michigan Stove Co., Stoves and Ranges; fine display; examine.
U and U.U, 17 and 18, Charter Oak Stove Co.—Examine Soft Coal Baseburner.
U and U.U. 19 and 20, Favorite Stove Works; examine.
U and U.U, 20 and 21, Buck's Stove and Range Co.
U and U.U, 22 and 23, William Miller & Co., Ranges; examine from other aisle.
Bet. U and U.U, 23 and 24, Colt's Fire-arms Co.; examine from next aisle.
Bet. U and U.U, 23 and 24, C. McKinnon, Pen Rest; examine it from next aisle.
Bet. U and U.U, 23 and 24, W. C. Bowers, Patent Fishhook; examine it from next aisle.
U.U, 25 and 26, Am. Machine Co., Hardware Specials, see samples; examine from next aisle.
U.U, 26, T. Fong, Japanese Goods; examine from next aisle.
U and U.U, 26 and 27, Colgate & Co., Perfumers; examine from next aisle.
Cross Main Aisle to U.U, 36, monumental Bronze Co.; examine.
U.U, 38, Freman's Face Powder.
U.U, 39, Pond's Extract.
U.U, 39, Weaver & Shandein, Perfumers.
U.U, 40 and 41, Griffin, Smith & Co., Pottery Manufacturing; examine.
U.U, 41 and 42, Albert Todd, Crystal White Essential Oils.
U.U, 42 and 43, Office of Baltimore *Sun*.
U.U, 43 to 44, C. Tiemann & Co., Brace Goods.
U.U, 43 to 44, G. R. Finlay & Co., Importers and Wholesale Druggists.
U.U, 43 and 44, in rear, D. N. Lebess & Co., Sponges.
U.U, 44 and 45, Stanley Works, Wrought-iron Butts.
U.U, 46 and 47, Powers & Weightman, Chemists and Importers; examine.
U.U, 47 and 49, I. L. Lyons & Co., Importers and Wholesale Druggists; examine immense Alum Crystal, 2,000 pounds, and Sponge Cup.
U.U, 50 and 51, Vail Bros., Ideal Tooth Powder.
U.U, 51, Fred. Stearns & Co., Manufacturing Chemists.

PRACTICAL COMMON SENSE GUIDE BOOK.   49

U.U, 51 and 52, Cheesborough Manufacturing Co., Chemical Products.
U.U, 52 and 53, Cibil's Beef Extract Co.
U.U, 53 and 54, Seabury & Johnson, Manufacturers of Plasters.
U.U, 53 and 54, T. W. Heinemann, Plasters, &c.
U.U, 54, Mosler, Bahmann & Co., Fire and Burglar-proof Safes, in rear.
U.U, 54 and 55, Kendall's Manufacturing Co., Soapine.
U and U.U, 55 and 56, Cincinnati Safe and Lock Co.
Turn around and view exhibits on opposite side of aisle.
T.T, 56 and 57, Clark, Herbert & Co., Fire and Burglar-proof Work, Safes and Vaults.
T.T, 53 and 51, Stein Manufacturing Co., Funeral Furniture; fine.
T.T, 51 and 50, Metallic Burial Co.; fine goods.
T.T, 49 and 48, J. H. Keller, Soaps; O. J. Keller in charge.
T.T, 47, Norfolk and New Brunswick Hosiery Co.
T.T, 47 and 46, Hutchinson, Pierce & Co., Star Shirt.
T.T, 45 to 44, Miss. Mills, Cotton and Woolen Goods; examine.
T.T, 44 to 43, Lehman, Abraham & Co., Cotton Mills.
T.T, 42 to 40, John Gauche's Sons, Crockery and House Furnishing; fine display.
T.T, 39 and 38, International Pottery Co., Trenton, N. J. See diamond chamberware, Japonica, Lotus ware, and celebrated porcelain dinner ware and hotel china.
T.T, 37, Empire Pottery Works, and Alpaugh and Magowan Pottery.
T.T, 36, Burroughs & Montford, Crockery.
T.T, 35 and 34, Union Pottery Works, Fine Decorated China.
T.T, 34 and 33, Ott & Brewer, Artistic Porcelain and Egg Shell Belleck; excellent display, and should be examined. Cross Main Aisle to
T.T, 31 and 30, Taylor's Premium Cologne.
T.T, 30 and 29, Swift Manufacturing Co., Bed Spreads.
T.T, 29 and 28, Thompson's Glove-Fitting Corsets, and Franklin Knitting Works.
T.T, 27, C. E. Mott, Florida Curiosities; examine.
T.T, 27 and 26, Fletcher Manufacturing Co., shoe-laces, &c. To left see American Machine Co.
T.T, 27, Amasa Lyon, Umbrellas.
T.T, 26, Hecht, Jewelry, &c.
Between T.T, 26 and 25, John Wyeth & Bros., Manufacturing Chemists.
T.T, 25 and 24, Randolph Paper Box Co.
T.T, 25 and 24, Parker Gun, Winchester Repeating Arms Co.
T.T, 24, Northfield Knife Co.
Between T.T, 23 and 22, William Simpson Sons & Co., Dress Goods.
T.T, 22, Barbour's Flax Thread; examine.
Bet. T.T, 21 and 22, Horstman Bros., Military Goods.
T.T, 22, Hough & Ford, Fine Shoes; Alaska Down Co., Bustles; L. & S. Sternberger, Shirts.
T.T, 19 and 20, John Bromley & Son, Carpets. See carpet-weaving.
T.T, 16 and 17, Wilmerding, Hoget & Co., Favorite Silk; examine.
T.T, 16 and 17, Le Grafs' Manufacturing Co., Boots and Shoes.
T.T, 17, Selz, Schwab & Co., Boots and Shoes; examine.

4

T.T, 16 and 15, Stribley & Co., Shoes; Marsop & Schottler, Fine Shoes.
T.T, 16 and 15, Cahill's Alma Shoe Polish.
T.T, 15, J. T. Marshall, Cuff-Holders.
T.T, 15 and 16.
T.T, 13 and 14, Goodyear Rubber Co; see shoe made in South America in 1821, and Chinese Rubbers.
T.T, 12, J. T. Hoffman, Worsted Store.
T.T, 12, Shriver & Co., Renewing of Crapes and Mourning Goods.
T.T, 11 and 10, Cassidy & Miller, Sailmakers and Cotton Duck.
T.T, 10, John T. Bailey & Co., Rope and Twine.
T.T, 9, Schlichter Jute Cordage Co.
T, 8, See this from next aisle.
T.T, 7, Fred. J. Myers Manufacturing Company, Wire and Iron Rope. (See from next aisle.)
T.T, 5, Johnston's Fluid Beef.
    Passing on toward end of building, see Corticelli Spool Silk, and the reeling of silk from cocoon.
U and T.T, 2, in rear of this, John Lucas & Co., Paints.
T, 5, turning back, Holmes & Coutts, Famous Eng. Biscuit.
T.T, 6, next, He-No Tea pavilion, where a cup of tea will be furnished you, free of charge. This pavilion is made of bamboo, and at night the dragon on top spouts fire from its mouth. Next, passing to
T, 7 and 8, see Doherty & Wadsworth Silk-Weaving; notice that the patterns control the harness, which controls the warp, and then the figure is largely made by the shuttle.
T, 8, Bakewell & Mullins, Manufacturers of Architectural Ornaments.
T, 9, August Benheim & Bauer, Clothiers.
T, 10, Chalmette Mills Fertilizers.
T, 12, A. G. Jennings & Son, Laces.
T, 13 and 14, A. Schwartz & Sons, Dry Goods; examine.
T, 15, Bonstein's Patent Pin Hook.
T, 15, B. F. Brown's French Dressing for Shoes.
T, 15, Andrew Bros., Boots and Shoes.
T, 16, Edwin Burt & Co., Boots and Shoes; excellent display; examine.
T, 17 and 18, Belding, Bros. & Co., Silk Manufacturers; fine display; examine crazy quilt.
T, 19, you examined from the other side.
T, 19, R. P. Hughes & Co., Importers of Feathers and Flowers.
T, 20, Rogers, Peet & Co., Rubber Clothing.
T, 20, Steel & Nissen, Fine Hats.
T, 22, Denny, Poor & Co., agents, Cloths; examine.
T, 24, Remmington Manufacturing Company.
Bet. T, 25 and 26, Bullard Repeating Arms Co.
T, 27, Joseph Beck & Co., Corsets.
T, 28, Coffin, Altimus & Co., Cotton and Woolen Goods.
T, 30 and 31, Meriden Britannia Co. Notice, in center, an opergne for banquets, value, $1,250; punch bowl, copy of one made for Dom Pedro, value, $1,092; ice-coolers, old Moorish style; the first is silver-plated; the second is gold-plated; the third is platina, making it iridescent; the decor-

ation is handwork, representing the cotton plant, blossoms, and balls, in front of which is the steamer "General Lee;" value, $300; at end of case, embossed set of four pieces, handwork, value, $255; old silver embossed tea set, with glass protector, value, $389; gold tea set, on nickel silver-ground, value, $575; near this, nickel silver-plated dinner set, value, $1,140; in corner of inside case, prize cup for a yacht race, value, $200; punch-bowl ladle, six goblets, and waiter, value, $225; near front, in outside case, Neptune fruit bowl and stand, value, $163; at rear of outside case, Cleopatra fruit stand, value, $375. Next beyond, in center of main aisle, is the mass of solid silver ore from Mexico, weighing 5,640 pounds, valued at $114,000. Now, cross the aisle to

T, 33 and 34, D. H. Holmes, Dry Goods. Rich display; notice white point d'aloncon, $35 per yard; another piece, white, handmade, same style, $80 per yard; gray, handmade, escurial lace, $30 per yard, and border $14 per yard; black escurial lace, over black satin, $30 per yard, and border $14 per yard (dress made and trimmed with these materials would cost $350); lace handkerchief, $60; white valenciennes lace, $45 per yard (it is over corn-colored silk); Duchess lace, on Nile-green silk, $45 per yard; valenciennes lace, on pink silk, $60 per yard; brocaded satin, with large flowers, $25 per yard; curtains, Brussels lace, $300 per pair; real Paisley shawl, $300. This display is subject to change.

T, 34 and 35, ——— ———, Inlaid Mosaic, Satin and Plush goods. Notice among mosaic work, "Regulus leaving Carthage," value, $250; fine plush goods.

T, 36, H. J. Mayers, for Mayer Bros., Majolica and Rockingham Ware. Notice, in front, pair of blue vases, value, $500; in rear, pair of brown vases; each leaf is formed separately.

T, 37, E. C. Penfield & Co., Celluloid Goods.

T, 38 and 39, ——— ———, Women's Work; examine.

T, 40, Ala. & Ga. Manufacturing Co., Cotton Duck.

T, 42, D. Danziger, Merchant and Manufacturer. (See Ship of Exhibits.)

T, 43, Clark's Mile End Spool Cotton.

T, 44, you have seen.

T, 46, Pomenah Mills Am. White Cotton Fabrics.

T, 46, Juan B. Stetson, Soft Hats.

T, 47, Brooklyn Shirt Co.

T, 47, Am. Hosiery Co., Fine Hosiery and Underwear.

T, 47 and 48, Empire Lamp Co.; T, 47, Am. Hosiery Co.

T, 48, Dunlap & Co., Hats.

T, 48, Canfield Dress Shield Co. Ladies, examine.

T, 49, Pittsburgh Arms Co. and Chamberlain's Cartridge Co.

T. 51, Philip Werlein, Mathushek Piano.

T. 53 and 54, Kranch & Bach Piano Co.

T, 55, Packard Organ Co.

T, 56 and 57, A. B. Chase Organ Co.

T, 58, Lee's Patent Ventilated Buckskin Undergarments.
  Here turn and take opposite side of isle.

S.S, 59, Young & Zerbe, Solicitors of Patents.

S.S, 56 and 57, Stieff Piano Co.

S.S. 55 and 56, Junius Hart, Pianos and Organs.
S.S. 53 and 54, John Schwab, The Connor's Pianos and Organs.
S.S. 50 and 52, Mason & Hamlin Organ and Piano Co.
S.S. 49, E. & M. Bollmann, Wine and Vinegar.
S.S. 49, John Moir & Son, Preserves, &c.
S.S. 44, Globe Pickle Co., and V. Blatz, brewer.
S.S. 44, Martin Kalbfleish & Sons, Wheat Baking Powder.
S.S. 43 and 44, Henry Moillard, Fine Confectionery.
S.S. 42, A. Colburn & Co., Mfrs. of Mustard and Laundry Blue.
S.S. 42, Carlton Blades, Coffees and Teas.
S.S. 41, Walter Baker & Co., Chocolate and Cocoa.
S.S. 39, Wolf & Relsing, Canned Fish, Lobster, &c.
S.S. 39, William Fields & Co., Embroidering Machines.
S.S. 38 and 37, P. C. Tomson's Potash, and Runkel Bros., Cocoas, &c.
S.S. 35, 36, and 37, D. Appleton, Books and Publications.
S.S. 34, Tomson & Houston Electric Co.; examine.

Here cross main aisle to

S.S. 31, A. J. Hohnan & Co., Publishers.
S.S. 30, Underwood's Chemical Writing Ink.
S.S. 30, H. Mahr's Sons, Mfrs. of Crown Filled Watch-case; examine.
S.S. 29, Lancaster Mills, Ginghams.
S.S. 27, Dwight Manufacturing Co., Cotton Goods, and Am. Hair Brush and Face Beautifier.
S.S. 26 and 25, E. A. Robinson, Manufacturer of Fine Plate-Rolled Jewelry.
S.S. 25 and 24, A. Erkenbrecker, Royal Gloss Lump Starch.
S.S. 23, Mitchell & Co., Old Irish Whiskey.
S.S. 22, King's Favorite Food—peculiar; examine.
S.S. 20, Speer's Favorite Wines, and Purdy & Nichols' Liquors.
S.S. 17, Bergner & Engel Brewing Co.
S.S. 17, Jarvis Brandy Co., Brandies.
S.S. 17, Am. Wine Co., Wines.
S.S. 15, Haraszthy & Co., Wines and Brandies.
S.S. 14 and 15, Philip Best, Milwaukee Beer.
S.S. 13 and 14, Schlitz's Milwaukee Beer.
S.S. 12, The Valentine Meat Juice Co.
S.S. 11, Bamer Packing Co.
S.S. 10, Maginnis' Cotton Oil Works and Soaps.
S.S. 9, Morris Tobacco Works; notice cascade, electrical railroad, and boat, bridge, mule, and cart; bladder of snuff on top of pyramid weighing 40 pounds.
S.S. 8, Durham Tobacco Manufacturing Co.; notice tobacco ship in motion; revolving pyramid; light-house; tobacco farm; railroad and mountain tunnel; granulated tobacco; the music you hear is playing "The Old North State."
S.S. 7, J. F. Donnell & Co., Lamps, &c.; fine display.
S.S. 6, Colgate's Soap.
S.S. 5, Erie Preserving Company.
S.S. 3, Dozier & Weyl Cracker Co.; examine.

Turning to left, see exhibit of
Bridgeport Wood Finishing Co.
R.R.S, 3, Helme's Snuff.
    Turn here to right to
R.R, 5, James Kirk & Co., Russian Soap.
R.R.S, 5 to 6, Kirk's Perfumery.
R.R.S, 8, Wm. Demuth & Co., Canes and Smokers' Articles.
R.R.S, 8 to 10, Allen & Gaiter, Manufacturers of Tobacco, &c.
R.R.S, 11, Magnolia Ham Co.; notice cute display.
R.R.S, 13, H. Clawson & Son, Brewers.
R.R.S, 14 and 15, Sunny Side Tobacco Co.
R.R.S, 16, Continental Brewing Co.
R.R.S, 16, The Cavarro Wine Co.
R.R.S, 18, Anheuser, Busch, Brewing Association.
R.R.S, 19, Purdy & Nichols, Importers of Cigars and Liquors.
R.R.S, 20, M. Wolf, Schnapps.
R.R.S, 22, E. J. Baldwin, Wines, &c.
R.R.S, 24, T. T. Hartel, Wines and Liquors.
R.R.S, 24, Craft and Allen, Confectioners.
R.R.S, 24, Reed's Gilt Edge Tonic.
R.R.S, 26, Pacific Mills, Dress Goods.
R.R.S, 27, Bill Brothers, Millinery.
R.R.S, 28, Shaw Stocking Co.
R.R.S, 31, Elgin Watch Co.; fine display; examine.
R.R.S, 33 and 34, Edison Light Co. See Chart.
R.R.S, 34 to 36, Harper Bros., Publishers.
R.R.S, 36 to 37, Jenney Electric Light Co.
R.R.S, 37 to 38, Berkley & Co., White Goods.
R.R.S, 40 to 41, A. Hahn & Co., Leather Goods.
R.R.S, 41, Arm & Hammer Brand Soda.
R.R.S, 42, Evan Hall, Sugar Plantation; examine.
R.R.S, 42, John Hallihan, New Canning Process.
R.R.S, 43 and 44, H. O. Wilbur & Son, Chocolates.
R.R.S, 44, Heinz Bros., Pickles; fine display; examine.
R.R.S, 46, Schmidt & Ziegler, Cigars.
R.R.S, 47, Boker's Stomach Bitters.
R.R.S, 48, Urbana Wine Co., Wines and Liquors.
R.R.S, 49, J. Eavenson & Sons, Toilet Soaps.
R.R.S, 49, California Chocolate Co.
R.R.S, 50 to 54, Ivers & Pond, Pianos.
R R.S, 55, Albert Krell, Violins.
R.R.S, 55, Gardner Piano.
R.R.S, 56, Sun Quog Wo, Chinese Goods.
    Now turn back to same aisle.
R.R, 59, East India Fancy Goods.
R.R and RR, 56 to 50, Grunewald Piano; fine display.
R.R and R, 49, Crane Bros., Paper Manufacturers; notice paper dome used as office, paper baskets, trays, &c.
R.R and RR, 48, W. L. Simons & Bros., Blank-books.

R.R and R, 48, Fairchild Gold Pen Co.
R.R and R, 47, J. W. Randolph & English, Blank-books.
R.R and R, 47, Whiting Paper Co.
R.R and R, 44, S. S. White, Dental Manufacturing; fine display.
R.R and R, 44, The Kruse Check and Adding Machine.
R.R and R, 43 and 44, William Mann, Blank-books. See large books.
R.R and R, 42 and 43, H. McAllaster, Stationery, Fancy Goods, &c.
R.R and R, 41 and 42, With E. C. Palmer, Holyoke Paper Co.; Carson & Brown, Paper Mfg.; Dennison Mfg. Co., Tags; George Bruce's Son & Co., Type Foundry; H. D. Wade & Co., Printing Inks; Estabrook Pen Co.
R.R and R, 41 and 42, E. C. Palmer & Co., Paper and Paper Goods and Stationery.
R.R and R, 40, George D. Barnard & Co., Blank-books.
R.R and R, 38 and 39, Waterbury Watch Co.
R.R and R, 37 and 38, Thomas Clock. This clock has a chime set on D B and G. First quarter hour, it strikes DB; second quarter, DB DG; third quarter, DB, DG, and DB; fourth, DB, DG, DB, and GB. Turning about here to,
R, 38 and 39, G. Sibley, Artificial Teeth.
R, 39 and 40, A. A. Marks, Artificial Limbs.
R, 39 and 40, J. H. Meyer, Dentistry.
R, 40, Hastings & Co., Gold Leaf. Now turn back to QQ. 37, and take that side of aisle, viewing exhibits to QQ, 44, not entering the Russian and Belgium Depts. Now—
R, 43, Byron Weston, Linen Record Paper.
R, 43 and 44, A. W. Hyatt, Printer and Lithographer.
Q.Q, 44, Ferdinand Vester, Olive Woods, &c.
Q.Q, 44 and 45, Anderson's Fruits, Butters, and Preserves; examine.
Q.Q and Q, 44 and 45, A. B. Kanny, Olive Woods.
Q.Q and Q, 46 and 47, Dr. J. Luby, Consulting Oculist.
Q.Q and Q, 47, J. H. Rushton, Sporting Boats and Sailing Canoes, &c.
Q.Q and Q, 48, Oriental Goods.
Q Q, 49, Jacob Touck, Articles from Holy Land and Egyptian Jewelry.
Q.Q and O.O, 50 and 53, Fairbank's Scales.
Q.Q and P.P, 54 and 55, Remington Agricultural Works; examine.
Q.Q and P.P, 56, Deere, Mansur & Co. Farm Implements and Machinery. Notice particularly double row corn planter, cotton and corn-stalk cutter, combined cotton and corn planter, and Gilpin sulky plow.
Q.Q and P, 58 and 59, Nichols, Shepherd & Co., Threshers and Traxtile Engines.

We are now in the Agricultural Section, which we will complete. It commences next to wall with
R.R, 62, Blount's True Blue Plows.
R, 22, J. S. Lamar, Cotton Cultivator.
R, 62. Farmers' Fertilizer Co., Lawn Dressing.
Q and Q.Q, 62, J. C. Semones, Bagasse Furnace.
P.P and P, 62, Cox & Poynter, Plows and Cultivators.
P, 62 and 63, the Vehicle Spring Co., the Chattanooga Wagon Spring.

O.O, 62, Superintendent of Agriculture.
O to N, 62, D. C. & H. C. Reed & Co., Harrows, Seeders, and Cultivators; examine.
N, 62, Hiram Holt & Co., Lightning Hay Knife.
N and MM, 62, Nash & Bro., Acme Pulverizing Harrow; farmers, examine.
K.K, 62, Henning Bros., Gas Machine; examine.
K. 62 and 63, Ewald Over, Ditching Plow and Road Grader; examine.
K.K and K, F. C. Romkey's Iron Harrow and Corn Cultivator.
H and I. 62, Brown Mfg. Co., Wagons and Cotton Cultivators.
H.H to F.F, 62, Produce Exchange.
F.F to F, 62, Wickes' Patent Refrigerator.
F and E.E, 62, Baldwin Dry Air Refrigerator.

Now turn to

F, 61, R. J. Walker, Ross Patent Refrigerator.

Turn to left, and go back in next aisle to

F.F, 62, American Live Stock Salt Roller Co.; examine.
G and G.G, 61, James L. Haven & Co., Royal Churn Power.
G.G and H.H, 61, E. W. Ross & Co., Feed Cutters.
I, 61, Foos Mfg. Co., Grinding Mills and Hand Power Blowers.
Bet. I and I.I, 61, St. Lawrence Mfg. Co, Harrows and Seed Drills.
I.I, 61, to L, 61, Hartshorn Double Spiral Spring Bed.
I.I, 61, P. C. Perkins & Co., Pumps and Windmills; these have an excellent reputation and should be examined.
H and K, 61, E. D. Carter, Cultivators.
K and K.K, 61, Dejan & Carter, Steak-tenderer.
K and K.K, 60, Rogers & Maher, Automatic Ice Cream Freezer.
L, 61, Hebner & Sons, Level Tread Horse Powers.
M and M.M, 61, Plano Mfg. Co., Draft Equalizer, and Johnson Harvester; should be examined by farmers.
N.N, 61, Johnson & Field, Fanning Mills.
O and O.O, 61, W. L. Boyer & Bros., Union Grain and Rice Thresher, Gristmills, Tread-mills, &c.
O.O to P, 61, A. W. Gray & Sons, Tread Power Threshers.
P.P, 61, Cleveland Carriage Goods Co.
Q, 61, Kemp & Burpee Mfg. Co., Trucks, &c.
Q, 61, Warren Fire Escape Co., Fire Escapes.
Q.Q, 61, The Hercules Mfg. Co., Wheat Scourer, &c.
R to R.R, 61, Homestead Fertilizer, and Dunn Edge Tool Co., and W. E. Canedy, Potato Planter.
R, 61, A. Riggs & Bros., Cisterns.
R to S, 61, John T. Noye Mfg. Co., Mill Machinery.
S.S, 61, Chess Carley Co., Fire Proof Oil; excellent exhibit; see process of boring and pumping oil, and representation of Pennsylvania R. R.

Now turn to

S.S, 62, Speer & Sons, Plows.
Q.Q, 59, Ivey's Adjustable Box for Wheel Vehicles.

The next you have seen.

Q, 59, Emerson, Talcott & Co., Agricultural Implements.
P.P, 59, Brown's Corn Planter Works.

P, 59, Charles T. Palmer, Leader Chilled Plow.
O.O and O, 59, The Globe Planter.
N.N and N, 59, Harron & Dexter, Clothes Washer.
N and M.M, 59, Davis' Fire Escape.
N and M.M 59, Dodge Manufacturing Co., Wood and Splint Pulleys.
M.L.L, and L, 59, James H. Hall & Co., Plows.
M, 59, to H, 59, B. F. Avery & Sons, Plows, Farm Implements, &c.; examine.
H, 59, to G.G, 59, Wisconsin Dairymen's Association.
G.G, 59, to G, 59, Simpson, McEntire & Co., exhibit of Wisconsin canned butter.
G.G, 59, to G, 59, Sheboygan Co., Dairy Board of Trade.
F.F, 59, to F, 59, Hutchins Refrigerating Car.
F.F, 60, Higgins Eureka Dairy Salt.
F.F, 59, American Salt Co. See figure of "Lot's Wife," cut out of salt rock.
F.F, 62, to F, 62, Refrigerators.

 Turning about here you have
F.F, 53 to 59, Cambria Iron Co.'s Exhibit. Come back to
G and G.G, 56, Cornish, Curtis & Greene, Dairy Goods; examine.
H and H.H, to I.I, 56, Thomas Meikel & Co., Steel Plows; fine exhibit. See miniature farm.
I to K.K, 56, McCormick's Reapers. See here original model.
K.K, 56, to M, 56, Buckeye Harvesting Machines; examine display.
M, 56, to N, 56, Birdsall Manufacturing Co., Portable and Traxtile Engines, Saw-Mills, &c.; examine.
N.N, 56 to O, 56, Pitt's Threshing Machines.
O.O, 56, to P, 56, L. Allen & Co., Manufacturers of Farming Tools.
P, 56, Q.Q, 56, Has been described; walk to next aisle and commence with
P, 54, R. Maltre, Seedman and Florist. Cross aisle to
O.O, 54, Cincinnati Water Elevator Co.
O, 54, Williams Tonsion Wheel Co.
O, 54, to N.N, 54, Michigan Scales Co.
N.N, 54, to N, 54, Owensboro' Wheel Co.
N.N, 54, to N, 54, Murry Iron Works, Meat Mixer, &c.
N.N, 54, to N, 54, Tichenor's Hand-Power Press, &c.
N, 54, to M.M, 54, Wrenn, Whitehurst & Co., Monarch Baling Co.

 Turning to right,
N, 56, Newark Machine Co., Seed Drills, &c.
M, 54, to L.L, 54, Superior Drill Co.
L.L, 54, K.K, 54, Kemp & Burpee Manufacturing Co., Manure Spreader.
K, 54, P. P. Mast & Co., Buckeye Cultivators.
I, 54, Whitman Agricultural Manufacturing Co., Agricultural Implements; examine.
 Now turn to
G.G, 52 and 51, Mavel & Williams, Cider Mills.
G.G, 51, American Well Works. Turn back to
H, 52, Frick & Co., Plowing Engines, &c.
I, 52, to K, 52, David Bradley Manufacturing Co., Plows; fine display; examine.
K.K, 52, Chattanooga Plow Co.
K.K, and L, 52, J. A. Field & Co., Sugar Makers' Supplies.

L, 52, Moline Plow Co.; examine.
M, 52, Howe Scale Co.
N.N, 52, Springfield Machine Co. and Springfield Manufacturing Co., Windmills, Pumps, Hay-rakes, Hay-tedders, &c.
O, 52, Buffalo Scale Co.
P to Q, 52, you have seen. Now turn to left in next aisle and go to
P.P, 49, Syracuse Chilled Plow Co.
P.P and O.O. 49, Albert Landon, Concentrated Salt and Columbian Marble Co.; examine. Fine display.
O, 49, Champion Iron Fence Co. Turn to right.
O, and O.O, 51, Osgood Scale Co.; examine.
N.N, 49, J. E. Stong, Excelsior Gate.
N, 49, Smith & Woodard, Eureka Windmill.
N, 49, to M.M, 49, George Burkhardt, Cedar Tanks
    Pass on to
L and L.L, 51, Thermostatic Incubator.
K.K, 49, Union Scale Co.
K, 49, Comstock Scale Machine Co.
K, 51, (To right,) Grover, Steele & Austin, Randolph's Grain Header.
I.I and I, 49, Harrison Machine Works, Engines and Threshers.
I.I, 49, (to left,) Western Wheel Scraper Co.
I, 49, Eagle Cotton Gin Co.
H.H, 49, Blymer Manufacturing Co., Engine and Sugar Mills and Bells.
G.G, 49, A. Schwartzwælder, Flour Mill Machinery.
G.G, 49 and 48, The Taylor Cottonseed Crusher and Grinder.
G.G, 48, American Scale Co., Automatic Patent Scale.
    Turn to left, and enter next aisle.
H, 44, to L.L, 47, (to right,) Pullman Car Co. Here you will see a miniature representation of the "City of Pullman," a suburban town of Chicago, where the palace-coaches are made. Prominent are Lake Calumet, the park, the water-tower, 200 feet high; all the various buildings connected with the car works; the arcade, 250×170 feet, containing 120 different kinds of stores; the cottages for workmen, &c. To the left of this exhibit,
I and I,I, 47, Allison Manufacturing Co., R. R. Cars, Car-fitting Boiler, Tubes, and Pipe.
K.K, 47, (on left,) Chamberlain Plow Co., and J. G. Tichner, Hamer Cotton Chopper. Next,
L, 47, (on left,) Deitz Automatic Fruit Evaporator, and J. F. Porter Steam Sugar Evaporator.
L.L, 47, S. E. & J. M. Sprout, The Bidwell Evaporator.
L.L, and M, 47, (next,) M. T. Hughes Evaporator. From
M.M, 47, to O, 47, The World's Exhibit of Vegetables, &c.; Grain in Straw, and, just beyond, the Flour and Meal Display.
O.O, 47, A. M. Johnson's Oat Meal Co. From
O.O, 47, to Q, 47, is the Mill Exhibit of the World, extending to
P.P, 44, Holmes & Co., Flour Display. See Minnehaha Falls.
O.O, 44, (next,) The Society for the Prevention of Cruelty to Animals; see exhibit. Notice illustration of the "Bell of Justice," and read card of explanation.

O, 44, (next,) North-western Terra-Cotta Works; examine.
N.N, 44, to M, 44, (next,) Grain Exhibit of the World. Turn here, and return to
Q, 44, and see R. W. Jackson, Abolone Shell Jewelry; wonderful display. This shell is found in no other place than San Francisco Bay. See mosaic table, worth $500; shell-framed clock, and California sea moss. From here you enter the Foreign Department, beginning with Russia, next to and adjoining Music Hall.

RUSSIA.

The principal exhibits from this Government are from St. Petersburg and Moscow, many of them being novel to most visitors, and should be carefully examined. Commencing with Q, 38 and 39, is the display of C. F. Woerffel, where you should notice particularly the following, viz: Beautifully painted wooden ware, made into almost every form, by the Russian peasants during the winter; next, the malachite tables, and same material in other forms—the largest table is valued at $1,500, the pair of large vases at end of large case, $800. Near these, see porphyry vase, valued at $1,500, laborite vase, valued at $250. With the malachite tables is one of lapis lazuli, valued at $500. Leaving these, turn to the Russian Bronzes, which are not only very wonderful, but instructive, as they represent much of Russian life. Each piece should be carefully studied. In front, notice piece, "The Russian Emigrants to Amour," valued at $500; "Market Peasant with Oxen," valued at $300; to the right, on case, are many of the designs, in bronze, of Prof. Lieberich, who was private sculptor to Alexander II. On top of case see "John, the Terrible," with his falcons; the "Russian Telaga," a peasant carriage with three horses. You will notice that their usual custom is to drive three horses. Passing next to P, 38, see paper maché work, which is not only beautiful and artistic, but illustrative of Russian life—the largest boxes are $50, the placques $5 to $10. Near this a piano from Moscow, on which see fine carving. Passing on to P, 37, see Russian Somovars in brass—these are for heating water for making tea; inside is a burner filled with charcoal, which is lighted from beneath; when the water is hot it is drawn from the faucet on the dry tea in the teapot, ready for use. The tea has no other steeping. Near this, see illustration of "running drosky," a sledge, and a "state sleigh," with a beautiful robe. Next, case of loaf sugar made from beets; to right, a case containing pillows, in gold or tinsel drapery, the large one is $50; the woolen pillow, and fruit and vegetable pieces were made by a lady 60 years of age, and are valued at $30, $40, and $50; next, large panel, on left side; set of laces, in case, valued at $600; just below, astrakhan cloth, $10 per yard; on opposite side gold tinsel or drapery (cotton ground) $10 to $15 per archine (Russian yard, of 28 inches); next, shawls of woolen, cotton, and woolen and cotton mixed, in bright colors; next, tulle lace, $9 per yard. At end of case, see artistic work cut with scissors, out of black paper, $15 each. On panel at M.M, 37, and M, 37, see tanned leather, including reindeer hide; on opposite side, high up, a cloth leather, very durable. In rear, notice several varieties of Russian droskies. Having reached the rear of Russian exhibit, turn to right, and enter the Belgium exhibit.

BELGIUM.

Upon entering this exhibit, you first reach the display of iron manufacture, which is worthy the special attention of all interested in that product. Next, is part of crockery exhibit, in which notice peculiar shapes; further along, additional crockery, where you will see some very pretty designs. To the right, in case, fine display of cotton and linen goods; next, glass goods, fine display; next, marble clocks; next, to right in cases, church goods; next to right, beautiful hand-made laces, one price, worth $2,000; next to left, the government geographical and museum display; next, to left, draperies on panels; next, to right, very fine display of 500 styles of cloths exhibited by Chamber of Commerce of Verniers; near front, beautifully carved bedstead, value, $1,500. In justice to this exhibit and myself, I state that when examination was made the exhibit was not complete. Leaving here, you pass directly back toward the rear or west end of building to the exhibits of R. R. Rolling Stock, street car, and traxtile engine and continue as directed in Guide immediately following.

You now enter upon the examination of Machinery Hall. To the right, in corner, are the great refrigerators and cold storage-rooms, and ice machine where ten tons of ice are manufactured daily; in front of this is the great filter, where all the water used in the buildings is filtered; next, is the reservoir, and arranged alongside of this are the force and ordinary pumps. The most of the exhibits in this section are of vast interest and should be visited by ladies as well as gentlemen. Your best course is to wend your way among the railroad, street car, and locomotive exhibits, to the Reservoir, and then pass to end of building to E. 62, pass along to corner of room, where you come to Refrigerator and Cold Storage-Rooms; pass alongside of building and refrigerator, until you reach the ice machines, which join the refrigerator: pass from ice machines to A.A, 54, where you take up the regular order of viewing the exhibits, until you come to platforms on which Engines are situated; then turn back and examine each aisle and the exhibits on the side of Engine Platform, which you are now on. Having finished these, cross platform by steps near side of building, and take up exhibits on other side of platform as indicated by Guide. I now continue the Guide in regular way, showing the particular exhibits with post numbers, which it will be well for you to consult as you proceed so as not to omit anything of importance.

D.D, 62, W. H. Brown Sons, Coal; see 8 and 10-ton blocks.

D, 62, Degraw, Aymer & Co., Oars. Hand-Spikes, &c.

B and B.B, 61 to 54, Cold Storage-Rooms.

B, 62, Ladies' Toilet.

} E, 60, to E, 56, } Cold Storage-rooms; back of this, Filter, Tanks, and Reservoir.
} B.B, 60 to 59, } servoir.

A.A, 63 to 54, Refrigerator, and Lunday, Smith & Co., Ice Manufacturers, making ten tons of ice daily, and cooling 12,000 cubic feet of space in Cold Rooms.

A.A, 50 and 51, John T. Smith, Boats and Oars.

A.A, 49, Knoxville Wheel Co., Car Wheels.

A, 41 and 43, French Spring Co., Car Springs.

A.A, 39, Carlisle Manufacturing Co.. Builders.

A. A, 38, Stillwell & Bierce, Steam Water Heater.
A. A, 36, Allen Paper Car Wheel Co. See paper car wheels
A, 35, A. Whitney & Sons, Car Wheels and Axles.
A, 34, Baltimore Car Wheel Co. See car wheels.
   Here turn back to
B, 34, Hancock Inspirator Co.
B, 36, Kœnig & Bauer, Lithographic Press.
B, 39, Boston Woven Hose Co.
B, 40 and 41, Burkey Foundry and Manufacturing Co., R. R. Hand Cars.
B, and B. B, 41 and 42, Alling's Lightning Dish Washer.
B, 43, Benj. Eastwood, Laundry Machine.
B, 44 and 45, A. M. Dolph & Co., Laundry Machine.
B, 46, Baily Wringing Machine Co.
B, 48, T. R. McMann & Bros., Heaters and Gas Fixtures, Radiators and Valves.
B, 50 and 51, H. D. Stratton & Co., Ice Machine.
   Turning back, to right in next aisle,
B. B, 48, G. M. Bickford, Babcock Washing Machine; examine.
B. B, 45 and 44, you have seen.
B. B, 43 and 42, you have seen.
B. B, 41 and 40, you have seen.
B. B, 38 and 39, Freeport Machine Co., Wind Mills and Feed Grinder.
   Now turn back to C, 34, and pass along to
C, 38, Prouty Power Printing Press Co.
C, 39 to 41, Huyett & Smith, The Smith Exhaust Fan.
C, 41 and 43, B. F. Sturtevant, Blowers and Drying Apparatus.
C and C.C, 43 and 44, Exhaust Ventilator Co., Ventilators.
C and C.C, 44 and 45, Detroit Blower Co.
C and C.C, 46, Combination Gas Machinery Co.
C and C.C, 47 and 48, B. W. Payne & Sons, Automatic Engines.
C and C.C, 52, J. W. Tully, Iron Filing and Steel Color Machinery Paints.
   Turn here to
D, 50 and 51, R. E. Deitz, Head Light.
D and D.D, 49, Excelsior Steam Pump.
D, 49 and 48, American Steam Gauge Co.
D, 48, Yunck & Co., Glass Blowers; see operation.
D, 48, James Barrett, Housetraps.
D, 48, H. C. Lowrie, Flushing Syphon and Housetraps.
D, 47 and 46, Ames Iron Works Co.
D, 45, A. Hanson, Inlaid Work.
D, 45, H. H. Thorp Manufacturing Co., Printing Presses.
D.D, 44, E. C. Palmer, Printing Presses.
D.D, 40 and 43, R. Hoe & Co., Printing Presses and Saws.
D and D.D, 39, Rayner's Challenge Pressure Filter.
D and D.D, 39, S. H. Quint & Son, Metallic Pattern Letters.
   Here turn to left and see display of the Reading Iron Co. Return to
D and D.D, 34 and 35, L. Graham & Son, Printing Machines, Type Materials.
   This completes Machinery Hall on this side of platform for engines, but before crossing, examine the largest of the engines. One of these, the "Rey-

nolds-Corliss," is of 650 horse-power; the other, the "Harris-Corliss," is of the same power. Their balance-wheels weigh 60,000 pounds each.

Passing over platform, you reach,
A.A, 31, Gandy Belting Co.
A.A, 30, N. Y. Belting and Packing Co.
A.A, 28, Chas. A. Schroeder & Co., Leather Belting, &c.
A.A, 28, J. B. Hoyt & Co., Belting.
A.A, 27, Boston Belting Co.
A.A, 27, Leviathan Belting Co.
A.A, 26, Maine Belting Co.
A.A, 25 and 26, Chattanooga Foundry Pipe Co.
A.A, 25, The Winn Boiler Compound.
A.A, 24 and 25. Cooper, Jones & Co., Gas Fitting, &c.
A.A, 23, James Leffel & Co., Mining Turbine Wheels.
A.A, 22 to 18, Coleman's Counter Shaft and Grist-mills.
A.A, 17 and 18, S. Chaffee & Burdenberg, Steam Governors.
A.A, 17, Watson's Portable Forge.
A.A, 17, Cincinnati Brass Co.
A.A, 16, Bergner & Co., Brick and Tile.
A.A, 15 and 14, Baltimore Bell and Brass Works.
A.A, 13, Hotchkiss Boiler Cleaner.
A.A, 13 to 12, H. W. Johns, Asbestos Cement.
A.A, 11 to 10, Eberhard Manufacturing Co., Carriages and Hardware.
A.A, 10 to 9, B. D. Wood & Co., Cast Iron Pipe. See pipe 6 feet in diameter.
A.A, 9 to 8, National Sheet Metal Roofing Co. Pass on to
A.A, 6 to 4, Blackmer & Post, Sewer and Culvert Pipe.
A.A, 4 to 3, Cincinnati Corrugating Co.
A.A, 3 to 1, Gents' Water-Closet. Turn about in same aisle to
B, 4, James Aikman & Co., Stamped Japan and Tin Goods.
B, 5, F. Armstrong & Co., Adjustable Stock and Dies for Presses.
B, 6, Henry Disston & Sons, Saws.
B, 8, Chapman Valve Manufacturing Co.
B, 8 and 9. Standard Lighting Co.
B, 9, C. Penilliat, Stair Work Machinery.
B, 10, A. W. Mason & Co., Machinery.
B, 11 and 12, Thos. Johns, Metallic Steam Packing.
B, 12, Medart Patent Pulley Co.
B, 13, Junius Jackson & Son, Steam Governors.
B, 14 to 15, Paige Manufacturing Co., Upright Boilers.
B, 11 to 17, H. Dudley Coleman, Fine display of Mining Turbine Wheels at work, a large Turning Lathe of 36 inches swing, Portable Engines, &c.
B, 25 to 29, Taylor Manufacturing Co., Fine display of Portable and Stationary Boilers. Passing here into next aisle on left, commence at
C and C.C, 31, American Wire Nail Co.
C and C.C, 31 to 28, J. W. Stevens & Son, Engines, Threshers, and French Burr Mills.
C, 27, Skinner & Wood, Engines and Boilers.
C, 25, Graphite Lubricating Co.
C, 24, The Altman-Taylor Thresher.

C, 22, Russell & Co., Stationary Boilers and Engines.
C, 18, A. H. Pomeroy, Scroll Saws and Scroll Sawing Materials.
C, 16, The Clark Gas Engine Co.
B.B, 13, (on right,) C. H. Delemater & Co., Hot Air Pumping Engines.
B.B, 12, Beandry & Cunningham, Upright Power Hammers.
B.B, 11 and 12, Rotary Nutmeg Mill.
C, 12 and 13, (On left,) W. J. Smith, The Buckeye Iron Grain Machine.
C, 11 and 12, The Powell Tool Co.
C, 12, Michigan Ax and Tool Co.
C, 10, P. J. Flanigan, Union Belt Fastening; and F. L. Grovet, Files.
B.B, 9, (to right,) Buffalo Forge Co.
C, 9, Eclipse Blacking Brush.
B.B, 8 and 9, (to right,) Wing's Disc Fan.
C, 7, (to left,) Atlantic Engineering Co.
B.B, 7, (to right,) Cleveland & Hardinwick, Engines.
C, 6, (to left,) American Machinery Co., Saw, Planer, and Knife-sharpener.
C, 5, C. W. Coes, Drill Presses.
B.B, 4, (to right,) Simond's Manufacturing Co., Saws.
B.B, 3, Mixter, Saw Tools.
B.B, 2, E. N. Walker & Co., Well-drilling Machinery.
C.C, 2, Morley Bros., Lumberman's Tools and Michigan Saw Works.
C.C, 2, E. T. Sufkin, Rule Manufacturing Co.
Now turn to left into next aisle and see
C.C, 3, E. C. Atkins & Co., fine display of saws. See one 86 inches in diameter, the largest in the world.
D, 3, (to right,) B. F. Scarfe & Sons, Manufacturers of Iron Buildings.
C.C, 4 and 5, (other side,) Jackson & Tyler, Machinery Tools, &c.
D, 4 and 5, (opposite side,) Laclede Fire Brick Co.
D, 5, Otis & Gorsline, Sewer and Drain Pipe.
C.C. 5 and 6, (opposite side,) Frank H. Morse, Barnes' Hand-sawing Machinery.
C.C, 6, Narragansett Machine Co., Foot Lathes.
C.C, 8, T. H. Bowers & Co., Collection of Patents.
C.C, 9, Austin, Opdyke & Co., Water Conductors.
Now pass on to
D, 12 and 13, (at right hand,) F. Rommarine's Bale Metallic Splicing Machine.
D, 13 and 14, National Sheet Metal Roofing Co., Metallic Shingles.
D, 14 and 15, the Pratt & Whitney Manufacturing Company, Machinists' Tools.
C.C, 14 and 15, (to left,) Myers, Osborn & Co., Oil Stoves and Ranges.
D, 15, (to right,) Louis Schwartz, Machinery Tools.
C.C, 16, (on left,) the Scoville Manufacturing Co., Boiler Feeder.
D, 19 and 20, and E. 19 and 20, Sugar Apparatus. Here you see the apparatus for sugar manufacture: first, the clarifier, in which the cane juice is clarified, from here it goes into the evaporating pan, then into the vacuum pan, in which the syrup is cooked to sugar. It next goes into the mixer, and from thence into the centrifugal boxes below, where the centrifugal motion throws all the molasses from the sugar.

D, 22, E. W. Bliss, Manufacturer of Presses, Dies, and other Machinery. Here turn to right into next aisle to

D, 24, Diamond, Emery Wheel and Machine Co.

D, 26, Dodge Manufacturing Co., Wood Splint Pulleys.

D, 27 and 29, Novelty Iron Works, Shingle Machine, largest in the world, one that cuts 150,000 a day. Here go to

E, and F.F, 24, where you will see the Edison Electric Light Plant, the largest in the world: it supplies some 18,000 lamps in the Main and Art Buildings. It is run by six automatic steam-engines, which drive twelve generators, which supply the electricity. As the ground is such that the ordinary foundation could not be laid, a peculiar frame-work was constructed, which notice. It sustains 200,000 pounds without vibration. Now turn back to

E, 28, Thompson-Lewis Electric Light.

E, 26, Plumley & Ritchie, the Heyle Suspension Hooks. Examine.

E, 25 and 26, C. A. Schmidt, Window Exhibitor.

E, 24 and 25, William Strange & Co., Silk Goods.

E, 22 and 23, William B. Fenton, Marble Working Machine; inlaid Tennessee marble center table; examine.

E, 21, Kalamazoo R. R. Velocipede Co.

E, 18, Iron Barbed Wire Co.

E, 16 and 17, A. W. Moffett, Band Scroll Sawing.

E, 14 and 15, Cooper, Hewit & Co., Steel Tablet Fence.

D, 13 and 14, (to right,) John A. Roebling's Sons, Steel Cable. Here is displayed immense steel cable used in Brooklyn and other bridges. The Brooklyn Bridge wire is composed of 6,000 seven steel wires, and its strength is 22,300,000 pounds.

D, 13, Variety Iron Works.

D, 12 to 10, F. A. Leigh & Co., Carding Engines. Now turn to opposite side.

E, 11, Cincinnati Barbed Wire Fence Co.

E, 9, B. F. Starr & Co., Flour Mill Machinery.

E, 8 and 7, Enterprise Manufacturing Co., Miscellaneous; examine.

E, 6 and 4, Nordyke, Harmon & Co., Mill Machinery; examine.

E, 3, George T. Smith, Centrifugal Flour Dressing Machinery. From here pass into machinery hall, "annex," where you may see various machinery at work, much of which is interesting. Here, too, will be the Cotton Mills exhibit, instead of in a separate building as was at first anticipated. On entering, you see first on right, Jillson & Palmer's Cotton Opener, and F. A. Leigh's Cotton Machines; first on left, S. A. Woods & Co., Planing and Matching Machines; second on right, Detroit Safe Co's exhibit; third on right, the Tennis Gang Flooring Machines; on opposite side, J. A. Fay & Co., Wood-Working Machines; on right again, Hall & Brown, Wood-Working Machines; next on right, Thompson & Houston, Electric Machines; on opposite side, Goodell & Waters, Wood-Working Machines; on right, Engle Cotton Gin Co.; opposite, H. B. Smith, Wood and Iron Working Machines; next on same side, A. D. Waymath & Co., Wood Turning Lathes; next, on same side, E. & F. Gleason, Tool Works; next on opposite side, Brown Cotton Gin Co., and Daniel Pratt's Cotton Gins; also other manufacturing companies, with cotton machinery: on opposite side, Smith & Myers, Engines and Saw Mills; next opposite side, Barbour's Cotton Gin; opposite side,

John White, Wood-Working Machinery; next, opposite side, Fulton Iron Works, Engines; next, Colwell Iron Works, all kinds of sugar machinery; next on opposite side, Frederick Stoltz, Scroll-Sawing; next on right in front, Remington Agricultural Co., Fiber Machinery; in rear, Benjamin & Fischer, Triumph Planer and Resawer; next on right, Rand Drill Co., Rock Drills; next on left, C. G. Pease, Wooden-Wedding Goods; next on left, The Forsaith Machinery Co,, who make here, and in large building of their own, just beyond this, a most wonderful display of a great variety of machinery, C. F. Gage, agent. Next on right, Morse Cotton Compress; next on left, M. Covel, Saw Sharpener, &c., new plan; next on left, Egan Wood-Working Machinery; next, S. C. Rutledge, Fiber Machine, near which is a machine for crushing and bleaching fiber, from N. Y. Ramie Fiber Co.; next, George Gibson's Fiber Machine, which strips the fiber. Now pass back into the machinery annex of "The Forsaith Machinery Co.," where an excellent display is made. After examining this, pass back of it, and examine The Sullivan Diamond Prospecting Drill, and its hydraulic feed, which regulates the cutting as desired. From this place is a walk to boat landing. Returning now to machinery hall "annex," pass along main aisle until you reach first principal cross aisle, in which, turning to right, you have patent boring and tenoning machines; turning to right, E. B. Holmes, Barrel and Stave Machinery; next, The Ryder Hot-Air Engines; next, Am. Diamond Rock Boring Co., here see core of rock bored out, 22 inches in diameter. Returning and passing cross aisle by which you entered this aisle, see H. L. Beach's Scroll-Sawing Machines; next, Gordon's Planer; next, American Hoop Dresser; next, James F. Curtis' Scroll-Sawing Machines. Pass along to first cross aisle to left, through which pass to main aisle and back to Machinery Hall, to E. E, 2, E. P. Allen & Co., Gray's Noiseless Rolling-Mills. Pass along aisle to

F and F.F, 4, Reading Bolt and Nut Works.

E. E, 5, (on left,) S. W. Tuft's Soda Water Machinery and Fountains; fine display.

F 5 and 6, (on right,) A. D. Puffer & Son, Soda Apparatus, which should be examined by persons interested.

E and E.E, 6, (on left,) Harden's Grenade Fire Extinguisher.

E and E.E, 7, Washburn & Moen Mfg. Co. See all kinds of wire and barbed wire made here. Fine display.

E and E.E, 9, The Gilbert & Bennett Mfg. Co., Wire and Wire Goods.

F, 8 and 9, (on right,) J. and P. Coats' Spool Cotton. Model of "The Old Stone Mill" at Newport, R. I., supposed to have been built by the Norsemen in the tenth century. The model is 12 feet high and 11 feet in diameter, and is composed of over 80,000 spools of cotton, with 153 shades of color. It is half the size of the "Old Mill," and is supported by eight columns, each a different color. Read quotation at top regarding it from Longfellow's "Skeleton in Armor."

E.E and E, 11, (on left,) Rose, Downs & Thompson Seed Oil Mill. This mill has been exhibited at Calcutta, India. See, also, Warmouth's Machine for shredding Sugar Cane.

F and F.F, 10 to 12, (on right,) F. Israel, Flour Mill Machinery.

F and F.F, 12 and 13, John T. Noye, Mfg. Co., Mill Machinery.

F and F.F, 14 and 16, Bridesburg Mfg. Co., Textile Machinery. Here are manufactured ginghams, bed-spreads, towels, &c.

E and E.E, 15 and 18, (on left.) U. S. Mint Exhibit. See coining of silver dollars, which requires some 100 tons pressure. They also make "Exposition Souvenirs."

F and F.F, 17 and 18, (on right,) August Gast & Co., Lithographing.

F and F.F, 17 and 18, A. W. Dowdell, Turning of Ivory, Bone, &c.

F and F.F, 20, (on right,) National Tube Works Co., Converse Lock-Joint Pipe.

F.F and G, 20 and 21, Kuemmerle, Vegetable Ivory Goods, &c.

F.F, 22 and 23, See manufacture of Gold and Silver Thimbles.

F and F.F, 22, G. and L. Brownel, Improved Cord-twisting Machine.

F and F.F, 23, American Pin Co. Turn here into next aisle to right, then commence on left with

F.F, 24, Henry Mitchell's Silk Mfg. See manufacture of handkerchiefs, with illustrations on them of the Exposition Buildings.

F.F, 25, Pioneer Silk Co.

F.F, 28, J. Mussey & Co., Silk Weaving.

F.F, 29 and 30, Hopedale Machine Co., Cotton Machinery. Now turn to opposite side of aisle to

G, 30 and 29, Cotton Mill Furnishing Goods.

G.G, 28 to 22, Whitin Cotton Machinery.

G and H, 21, to G and H, 19, Clark's O. N. T. Spool Cotton. See automatic machine which winds over 6,000 spools a day, taking 8 spools at one time, fastens the thread on each, and winds 200 yards on each, stopping immediately at the termination of the 200 yards. It then makes a slit or incision on the edge of each spool, and fastens the thread in it, cuts off the thread, and drops the spool. Next see the stamping process, which is done by hand; one young lady stamps 30,000 spools a day. Also, see monster 100-mile spools of cotton. The case, which stands 20 feet high, cost about $2,000. Jars in which they test the color of their thread by oxalic, nitric, and other powerful acids.

G.G, 17 to 7, The Willimantic Cotton Co. Stepping upon platform, see to your left in small room, the spool-machine, which makes some 22,000 spools a day. Back of this, the wonderful braid-machine, which makes all kinds of braid, specimens of which you see here. You will notice that one bobbin has a piece of paper on it. Now, by watching this bobbin you can see just what the movement of each one is. So delicate is this machine that it will use No. 100 thread, and at the breakage of one thread only, the entire machine will stop. Now, you pass on and see the process of spool-cotton manufacture. The cotton used in making the thread is Sea Island, (the best,) and the process which it passes through in general, as follows: 1st, picking to remove seeds and dirt; 2d, carding to arrange the cleaned fibers parallel; 3d, the drawing out process, which is the running of the fiber between two sets of rollers, one set running faster than the other, thus drawing out the fiber, which is done by several operations, with different machines, as you will see here. After a few drawings, the fibers are called slivers. These slivers are put together in another machine, to comb them again, so as to remove any foreign substance and short fibers, and it is again

5

drawn out. Next commences the twisting of fibers, which, at first, is slight, called "roving;" then it is drawn and doubled again, making six cords in one. The next process is "spinning," which is a simultaneous drawing and twisting. To accomplish all this, together with spooling and stamping, this company have nineteen processes, as follows, viz: 1st, picking; 2d, carding; 3d, reducing, or drawing out with rollers; 4th, lap-winder, which takes fourteen strands, or fibers, and winds them together; 5th, comber, for removing all foreign substances and short fiber; 6th, drawing, which takes the fourteen fibers and reduces or draws them to size of one; 7th, drawing or reducing and twisting slightly; 8th, drawing and twisting slightly again; 9th, draws, twists, and winds on bobbins; 10th, spinning; 11th, two cords doubled; 12th, twisting these two cords into one; 13th, winding on bobbin; 14th, uniting three of the two cords, that is, doubling and making the six cords of the thread; 15th, twisting the new cord; 16th, reeling; 17th, placing on swift for spooling; 18th, spooling; 19th, ticketing. There is one process which cannot be shown here, which comes after the 16th process, (reeling,) and that is the whitening or coloring, for which it is sent to the dyer's. In large case at end, see pyramid of spool-cotton, composed of 22,000 spools; also, large spools, each containing 12,000 yards; in front of other long pyramidal case, see illustration of all methods used among Chinese in working cotton; also, inside of case, see specimens of cotton in every form, from raw cotton in seed up to the different forms of manipulation, and the waste by the side of each specimen. Pass on to

G.G, 5, John Mathews, Soda Water Apparatus.

Now, turning to left and taking opposite side of same aisle, see

F.F, 5, Weikel & Smith Spice Co.

The next you have seen.

F.F, 10, (next,) Wonderful Collection of Petrified Trees, from Desert of Arizona. See how it polishes.

F.F, 11 and 12, (next,) Waterbury Button Co. Here they are making buttons and putting pins on a paper by machinery.

F.F, 12 and 13, you have seen from the other side. Pass to

F.F, 15 and 16. See the Roller Mill, and process of making New Process Flour, J. T. Noye.

F.F, 17, Glass Engraver.

F.F, 18, The Phœnix Silk Manufacturing Co. Here they make Exposition Souvenirs. Now pass along aisle till you reach G.G, 28, at which place turn to right, through aisle to H, 28, where you reach the Foreign Department. Turning to right, you enter Austria, commencing with the wonderful Bohemian Glass Exhibit of Ludwig Moser. Notice particularly, as follows, viz: Beautiful vases on case, $450 per pair; set (3 pieces) on opposite case, $450; cut-glass fruit dish, high up on case, $500; vase by it, $450; lamp near this, $150; also near by, a pair of vases, $450; punch set (bowl and 7 glass), beautiful, $480; enameled glass, wine-color and white, vases (hand-work), $250; blue enameled vases, opposite, $200; punch bowl, in blue and gold, decorated, $225; three card stands, $225. Leaving here, follow posts numbered 27, examining the exhibits on line of posts 27 and 28, and continue on to Q Q, 25 and 26, and Q, 27. I now give these exhibits in their order.

M, 25 and 26, Haing Chong, China Ware and Japanese Curiosities.

M.M, 26, Francis Walch, Bohemian Glass, including the celebrated Count Harrach's Bohemian Glass. See fine pair of vases on top of case, worth $500; beautiful display of Austrian Jewelry and genuine gems, including an immense pearl.
M.M, 27, Michael Goldschmidt & Son, Real Bohemian Goods.
N, 27, Schreppel & Walch, Meerschaum Goods and China Flowers.
N, 27, Maurice Taussig, Imitation Gems; examine.
N.N, 25, Raimond Nagl, Amber Meerschaums.
O, 25, H. M. Dodany, Inlaid Mosaic Wood Work; examine.
O.O, 27, S. Veit, Manufacturer of Jewelry and Lapidary; examine.
Next toward front, the furniture display (bent goods) of Thonet Bros., of Vienna. Notice particularly lady's dressing mirror, in dark mahogany, (new style;) a gilded set, composed of four chairs, two arm chairs, and sofa, upholstered in black silk; parlor chair, No. 1, very beautiful; a rocking arm chair, with fine upholstering. Turning to the right, enter Italy.

ITALY.

Upon entering this exhibit, first in front, you will see the fine display of F. Errico, of Italian bronzes, Naples artistic work, including silver filigree, tortoise shell, lava and coral work, and jewelry, majolica, vases, &c. Notice particularly the following, viz: Two large bronzes in front, $250 and $350, respectively; fishermen and boat, (hand made); Pompeiian bronze; pair of scales; a bronze "Minerva;" bronze candelabra, $250; hand-carved lava work, in case; photographic illustrations in Venice, including Rialto, &c. Next, Q, 24, Alla Farfalla, Venetian Goods; examine. Continuing on, carefully examine the displays at P.P, 24, P, 24, and O, 24, as they contain fine and varied exhibits of Italian manufacture, especially Venetian Goods. First after this, J. E. Canini, Venetian Glass and Wooden Statuary, fine display, which should be examined. Next, R. E. Brunacci, Roman Jewelry, Inlaid Olive Woods, Florence Mosaics, and Venice China Jewelry, fine display, and should be carefully examined. Next, M. Labriola, large variety of tortoise and conch shell work, Venetian glass. Notice in tortoise shell work the difference in beauty and value between the light and dark colored shell, most noticeable in display of fans, which are beautifully hand-painted. Next, Achile Olweri, mosaics, cameos, coral and filigree jewelry, and Venetian glass. Notice particularly beautiful filigree, cameo, and glass work. Next, Olwoti Brothers, majolica, mosaics, Venetian glass, Venetian photographs. Notice particularly beautiful mosaics, pretty majolica, and peculiar terracotta. Next, Gioni Boncinelli, Florence mosaics and bijoutry; fine display; examine. Next, Antonio Mari, glass engraver. Next, Michele Griscuolo, cameos, coral, &c.; jewelry; beautiful exhibit of mosaic and filigree; fine display. Notice particularly his Egyptian and Arabian styles of jewelry, and his illustration showing the mode of coral fishing, which none should fail to see. Next, M. Valsecchi, fine filigree work. Next, Di Mariano & Co., diamonds and fine jewelry; beautiful display; examine. Next, Garobolo & Co., delicate and beautiful jewelry; examine. Next, Graziotie Petoreto, Florence mosaics, Roman filigree work; very peculiar exhibit; don't fail to see. Now turning to left, you enter France.

FRANCE.

Beginning with I & I. I, 20, Decauville's Portable Railway, for use at mines, &c., samples of track and cars. This road may be seen in actual operation at the Mexican Gardens.

H. H, 22, J. Neiter & Prestat, Patent Enameled Mirrors, fine display; examine; the largest one worth $400.

L. L, 22, L. Lacroix, Cigarette Paper. Notice one roll containing 6,000 yards, and one of 4,000 yards.

M and M. M, 20, A. Luez, French Diamonds.

N. N, 20 and 22, R. Pouvier, Porcelain Flowers; examine. Next, F. Rnmine, Porcelain Articles and Imitation Dresden Ware and Antique Glass with pearls. Notice little coffee set, $50.

Q and Q. Q, 20, Kaffel & Freres, Artistic Chiseled Bronzes, Paintings, and Ceramics. Notice particularly, as follows, viz: A porcelain stand in Louis XVI style, artistic chiseling, value, $400. In front, a vase on stand, hand-painted Sevre. The painting is on enamel, which is baked in a heat of 800 degrees; then the gold decoration is applied, and cooked at crystal fire. These are $600 per pair. The mate to this one is on opposite side, and should be contrasted with the first, as each presents two different faces, giving four different faces in the pair; and notice the exquisite chiseling upon them and varieties of color of gold, which are the matte, the mercury, the green, and the yellow. Next, the blue Sevre vase, or Gros-Bleu, after the school of Watean; examine both sides. The bronze ground-work of the metal ornamentation is chiseled after the school of Odiot; the cupids are exquisite; value, $200. Next, a lady of the middle ages, painted on Faïence, in enamel, and burned twice, each burning of six hours; value, $100. Charlemagne, in same work; Cachemere marble stands, very beautiful and transparent, showing every color of the rainbow, classical style of Louis XIV; value, $500. Decorated clock, representing Æsop's Fable of the "Crane and the Fox," value, $90; toilet table in Pompadour style, value, $350. Among placques, see fine porcelain placque of dogs, painted porcelain screen, very fine, value $180.

P. P, 20, M. M. Lafargue & Brierre. This firm represents a large number of houses in France, and makes a fine display of Art Bronzes, Religious Statues, Religious Jewelry, Stained Glass, Tapestries, Mechanical Dolls, Shoes, and Corsets, &c. Notice, particularly, as follows, viz: Among religious statues, a church, Sacred Heart, Montmartre, Paris, and a model of statue representing "The Prayer for France"—the pope, France, and above, the Saviour, this statue is to be placed in the church; notice the wonderful expression in the eyes of "France." Next, St. Paul de Vincent, the great philanthropist of France; holding child in one arm, and leading another; next, beautiful stained church glass, 20 feet high; next, China flowers. Among bronzes, in front, notice Sepoy slaves, value, $2,500 a pair; near here, vases, value. $225 each ; bronze and onyx vase, value, $225 ; "Commerce, Industry and Peace," value, $1,150 ; "The Boy and Cat," value, $175 ; in rear, Louis XIV vase, value, $750 ; near this, Renaissance vase, value, $550, a copy of the original at Fontainebleau ; on other side, "The Steeple Chase." value, $375; next, back, embossed leather furniture, largest chair, $60 ;

next, back, fine boots and shoes. In large case at right, wonderful mechanical dolls ; back still farther, fine display of artistic and expensive tapestry in all styles; at the right, on the other side, is a beautiful exhibit of ceramics of the most artistic styles and finish, and high value, and should be carefully examined. As fine a collection is seldom seen, and it should not be passed with a glance, but carefully viewed. Directly back of this, notice Don Quixote, Sancho Panza, and others, made of paper mache, in imitation of bronze. Finishing this, turn to left and enter England, next to Miscellaneous Department.

ENGLAND.

Q, 17, Entering this exhibit at this post number, you first see slag ware, made from the slag which is taken from iron ore smelting. This illustrates how useful millions of tons of heretofore considered worse than useless material may be utilized.

P, 17, Here are various displays, among which are fruit jams, canned meats, &c., but the most interesting display is of the Donegal Testimonial Fund, which includes largely laces made by poor Irish peasant women. This collection is for sale, and the proceeds are to be charitably distributed among these poor workers. Next, is an exhibit of Row-locks and Thole-pins for boats, most excellent, and should be examined by all interested in this direction.

M. M, 17, to K. K, 17, Felix & Wayman, French and English Artists, in upholstery, cabinet-making, decorating, &c. This exhibit represents one of the great London houses, which makes a wonderful display—one seldom seen—and none should fail to see it. Entering from the front, the first room you view is furnished in style of Louis XVI, with the finest furniture and furnishings made in England. Notice particularly the screen in imitation of Dresden china, a new style, only two have ever been made—the other for the Princess Louise, in Kensington Palace ; the four chairs, each different—notice perfection in carving; the brass work is chased and then gilded ; the furniture painting is Verin Martin, (a new discovery,) the secret and beauty of which lies in its perfection of surface. From any roughness of surface no paint can be detected. The carpet is an Aubusson—the finest carpet made—and is worth $1,000. The sunshades are of festooned silk, of the latest pattern. A room furnished in this style would cost from $10,000 to $15,000. The curtain you see at side is one hundred and fifty years old, and was made by Genoaese Nuns. The wrought-iron candelabra is valued at $1,000. The second room is furnished with two bed-room sets—one is mahogany and painted coiffier, hand-painting, fourteen pieces, worth $2,500 ; the second is inlaid mahogany—here see white oak side-board in Renaissance style, worth $1,500 Notice illustration of giving to wood an old appearance. It is done by placing it in an oven with spirits of ammonia. The third room, finest of all—notice here fine panel work. The two side pieces of Verin Martin, (the new method of painting,) one made for the Princess Louise, worth $1,700, the other worth $1,200. The red velvet screen was made for the wife of one of the wealthiest bankers in London. The window drapery, in yellow brocade—the two sets are worth $1,500. Around the room are fine specimens of Axminster carpets, which this firm manufactures. They manufacture carpets of any size desired. The total value of this exhibit is between $30,000 and $40,000. All of this display is for sale. Stepping around to rear of the exhibit, you will see specimens of the finest English wall paper. Turning here to 11. H, 15, you reach Jamaica.

JAMAICA.

In the exhibit from this island, notice particularly, as follows: A pair of large grain corals; table of cocoanuts, the outside covering of which is called "coir,"—see fiber made from it, of which cocoa matting is manufactured; observe, near table, the small cocoa-palm, and the peculiar way it thrusts itself through the shell, where it subsists on the cocoanut inside until it actually absorbs all the meat of the cocoanut; on the other side, 200 medicinal plants, among which notice the cocoa-leaf, a local anæsthetic, discovered within the last year. Before an operation is performed, this cocoa-leaf can be applied to the part affected, where it will destroy all sense of feeling without injury to the person. It was recently applied to General Grant. At end of exhibit, notice in tub of water, rock coral; see method of extracting perfume from tube roses and other flowers, which is done by laying them on lard, underneath a cover. The perfume is absorbed by the lard, which is sent abroad and prepared for market. Samples of rum, some 30 years old; among woods, notice a bitter wood, which is used, in place of hops, for making beer; in case near by, see lace and lace work made from the lace bark tree; table of canned fruits, which are labeled, among which observe nutmegs—1st, the green pulp; 2d, the mace; 3d, the nutmeg; on the other side, different machine-dressed fibers, labeled. Photographs of buildings on the island. Leaving Jamaica, you next enter Siam.

SIAM.

This exhibit consists of all grades of cotton goods, woven by women. Notice particularly, as follows, viz: The Siamese loom; shuttles; cotton-field implements; cotton-carding brushes; hoes and models of the skein reel; cop winder; cotton rolls; crank and spiral gear; crank and treadle; showing that nearly all of their implements used in the raising and manipulation of cotton are very rude. Yet this country is one of the richest in the world in the variety of its production, and yields the most luxuriant crops of cotton. Continuing on, you next enter the German Department.

GERMANY.

Entering this department, pass along to P, 15, Albert Uebele. Fine exhibit of Sterling Silver and Precious Stone Jewelry, which will repay examination. Next, P.P, 15, Tittle Kruger, Fine display of Worsted Work. Turning to right, you reach the Republic of Honduras.

REPUBLIC OF HONDURAS.

In this exhibit, among grains, notice particularly a peculiar wheat, the chocolate beans, coffee plant, with the fruit before it is chucked; specimen of gutta-percha, and gum made from it. Among the woods, notice the Brazil wood, balsam wood, rose wood. Near this wood see cochineal insects. Among the brandies, wines, &c., a brandy made from sugar-cane, and wine made from cactus, (*agua de vejuco.*) Around pagoda in center, school work in Spanish, Indian relics, with section of comb-tree. Also notice the coins which they use. Next you enter Japan.

JAPAN.

This exhibit is made up of the Government exhibit, in which is also wonderful display of the Nipon Merchantile Co. of Tokia, and adjoining, exhibit of Misan Kaisha, of Kioto, Japan. Each of these exhibits is very fine, and attention can only be called to the most beautiful and expensive articles. In the Govt. Ex., notice particularly in case fine collection of bronze vases inlaid with gold, one pair worth $900; also a single vase valued at $650, and with these a small box, valued at $150. Near here is a bronze piece representing tree trunk and eagle, valued at $450; another, with lotus flowers inlaid with gold, $325; a pair of blue and white Koransha porcelain vases, valued at $1,200; one Koransha porcelain vase in gold relief, value $900; a Satsuma Incense Burner, value, $650; metal placque, $150; Cloissonne-work vases, standing on case, eighteen inches high, value, $550 a pair; wood panel inlaid with ivory, on case, value $250; Koransha porcelain placque, three feet in diameter, value, $250; near this, silk pattern, $150.

Among screens, see one in gold, $150; a six-fold screen, in silk and gold, $350; decorated china, shell cup and saucer. The display of Meisan Kaisha in the adjoining exhibit is of great interest, and contains some very rich wares. Notice particularly the fine bronzes, in case near center, inlaid with beaten gold; the largest pair is valued at $1,600; it took one man six years to make it; the figures represent antique designs controlled by the emperor, which are over two thousand years old; cloissonne enameled vases—there is only one artist who makes this elegant work; it has to pass through from seven to ten processes; in large case back of this, see iron vase inlaid with gold—it took five years to make it, and is valued at $1,200; in this case, also, set of vases, (3,) hand-painted porcelain, valued at $1,000; screen, in same case, made expressly for this Exposition, representing the cotton plant, value, $250; also a bed spread finished with gold, value, $150; near this a pair of curtains, value, $150; hand-made lace, said to be equal to Brussels, among which is a handkerchief valued at $105, and a set of laces valued at $305. Lace-making is a new interest in Japan. See bamboo cases and bamboo work in all shapes; silk toys. In alcove at end of pavilion, see ancient armor; raw silk; telegraph instrument manufactured in Japan; bamboo and bead screens; hand-painted paper screens, value, $50; silk screens, value, from $10 to $50; plate of Satsuma ware, value, $75; beautiful porcelain ware, to right—cute porcelain tub, $50; tea-pots, from $15 to $50, (hand-painted.)

CHINA.

This exhibit is almost purely a cotton display, made expressly for the Centennial, but still it has, perhaps, even greater interest on that account, as it is complete in all respects. The seed is planted in April. Their plow is a crooked branch, with a thin iron plate attached. The tilling is done with a three-pronged hoe. Specimens of these and all cotton machinery, and illustrations of their working, can be seen, and should be carefully examined. Notice particularly as follows, viz: Various customes as illustrated by dummies. A bride of common class in winter costume; a widow in mourning. Her dress is white, and in her hand she carries the "mourning stick." The period for mourning is three years, but practically it is reduced to 27 months. Mandarin and accountant; Buddhist Priest, with yellow robe and scarred head to mark his calling; irrigating pumps, worked by men and oxen; interior of a dye-house; cotton gin; the flocking-bow, which is struck by a man with a mallet, thus loosening and spreading the cotton so it may be used for quilts, &c; cotton spinning wheel, invented by a woman, from which three threads are reeled; machine for preparing yarn before it goes to loom; cotton loom; cotton press; brown cotton, from which "nankeen" is made; mixed cotton and silk goods; cotton clothes of various colors and quality; cotton lining, in imitation of lamb's wool; cotton and silk velvets; Chinese houses and boats; boots and shoes; case of ivory carving; wonderful grass cloth, sold at 50 cents a yard; woolen goods; inlaid furniture and screen inside of house; bamboo work in every shape and use. This (bamboo) is China's iron. She makes her knives, or chop sticks, houses, and nearly every thing else of it. Bed quilts with silk finish; bamboo jackets, to prevent the clothing from touching the body in warm weather.

BRITISH HONDURAS.

This exhibit comprises mostly native woods. Notice, particularly, fine display of mahogany, in wood and in beautiful case—bath tub; native fish trap, on top; case of pre-historic relics; pile of log wood, in corner; a wooler, or strainer, on post, for straining cassava; three inlaid tables of native woods, very beautiful, the largest one is valued at $125; Pitpan or Canoe used on rivers; native rubber; also large logs of mahogany and cedar. Turning to left, you enter the Central American States. Pass along and examine these until you reach Guatemala.

GUATEMALA.

This republic lies in the tropical belt and all her agricultural exhibit is of tropical productions. Notice, particularly, the following, viz: The altitude at which most of her productions are raised, 4,000 feet and upwards. In first pyramid of seeds, grains, &c., the large kernels of coffee. The production of this staple is large and fine, and the Republic desires to call the attention of American merchants to the fact. Cocoa beans, from which cocoa and choco-late are made. Further along, on side table, vegetable tallow, made from the beans of tallow tree, (see samples,) used for candles, &c. Still farther along, see fiber of maguey; India rubber; sea beans, which are a nut carried to sea by the river; incense, a gum taken from the incense tree. On next pyramid of seeds, &c., see red beans, peculiar wheat; see raw hide of the manitee or sea cow. Near this, Indian goods. At end of exhibit, among birds, see the wonderful "Liberty," very beautiful, and so proud of its plumage that at a loss of one feather, or deprivation of its liberty, it dies. Here see portrait of President Borrios, of the Republic, one of the ablest and most enterprising of the public men of Central America. In center of this part of the exhibit and between tables, see bunch of straw from which Panama hats are made. From here, turn to Mexican Exhibit, which enter at P, 8.

BRAZIL.

The exhibit from this empire is made by the Association of Commerce, of Rio Janeiro, for the purpose of showing to the world that much of the coffee which is sold for genuine Java and Mocha is really Rio Coffee. The association shows coffee from 624 plantations, which are all numbered. There are 624 qualities of Rio, equal to 50 grades, and in this large exhibit they will show you the different coffees sold as Java, as follows: 493, 510, 176, 38, 39, 52, 353, 547, 508, 211, 214, 356, 398, 233, 216, 141, making 16 qualities. Those sold as Mocha are as follows: 186, 619, 620, making 3 qualities. Now turn to the right and enter Mexico at P, 8.

MEXICO.

Entering this exhibit at P, 8, you will notice that it is arranged so as to form courts. Beginning in this court, next to Miscellaneous, with cases on your left toward front, you see the wood fibers of Mexico; next, the cloths made from them, which show the quality, and should be examined; next, leather and goods made from it, and near here notice the down of the pelican. At outside corner, next to Miscellaneous Department, see alligator hide, and another long one, which is a viper's hide. Next, the elegant saddles, some of which are silver-mounted, and cost as much as $900. Passing around to case on other side of this court, you should carefully examine the excellently tanned and colored leathers, for this is one of the finest features of this wonderful exhibit. You will see that it is dressed and colored in imitation of a great many patterns of cloth. That which you might at first suppose to be cloth is actually leather. Turning now to woods in center of court, see large section of cedar, five feet in diameter, and an immense tub, cut out of same wood, showing how they make these articles; also, trunk, or box, of a beautiful perfumed wood, which always retains its perfume, and is very rare; another box of the most precious woods of the tropics; wonderfully carved picture-frame. Passing on to the table of minerals in this court, you see exhibited building stones, including marbles; among these, notice, also, red semi-circular tile, used for roofing, and on top of case, flat tile used in building. The white, cone-like formations you see are water-filters, hollow. The water is poured in, and permeates the material, dripping through pure and cold. The large knives, near here, are used for cutting sugar-cane. The cases on each side are filled with wonderful Indian work; the pottery is remarkable, and of fast colors; also, examine the cloth made from a silk bark, nearly as soft and fine as silk. Turning to left, enter the next front court, Q and P.P, 5, in which are woolen and cotton manufactures, including shawls, bedspreads, mantillas, and the robozo, which is a long, narrow shawl, used for wearing both over the head and shoulders. These are made of all qualities, of both cotton and silk, but the finest are generally cotton, costing as high as $150, and made of No. 200 cotton, of the most beautiful colors. They are so finely woven that they may be drawn through a finger ring. Here see table of inlaid work, valued at $180. Now enter next court, O.O and O, 5, in which you find wools and cottons, including a brown cotton, which is its natural color; cotton and woolen goods, including fine cassimers; two earthen vases, in imitation of ancient Aztecs.

Notice particularly here a blanket decorated with Mexican and U. S. Flags, in case on left. Next court, N and M.M, 5, contains exhibit of City Hospital of Mexico; government army exhibit; government mail service, and uniforms of police of City of Mexico, fire company, &c. Now, turning to right, examine the furniture display by a merchant in the City of Mexico, where notice a bed-room set of Scripture wood, very hard and much finer than mahogany, valued at $5,000; side-board of ebony and inlaid woods, valued at $1,500; cabinet of inlaid woods, value, $500; carving, 250 years old, taken from an old church; cabinet of tiger wood, a hard and expensive wood, value, $500; specimen of dining-room flooring, 20 × 40 feet. Beyond this, and to left, is the monument of polished woods of Mexico, 40 feet high, which contains a different wood every two inches. Next court, M.M, 5, you notice an embroidered piano stool, value, $104, and near it gold embroidery, value, $40; near this, cases filled with Mexican onyx in the shapes of all Mexican fruits; this onyx is a species of chalcedony, or uncrystallized quartz. In next court, M and L.L, 5, Mexican marbles, and at L.L, 5, antiquities and casts of antiquities. In next court, K.K and K, 5, to left, books and publications, including a Mexican City newspaper and one edited by a woman. On the other side see shell work, onyx, woods, and Lower California birds. In next court, I and H.H, 5, you have every kind and form of liquor made from the maguey, wines, and sugar from cane; some in cakes, you will observe, resembles the maple sugar. In next court, I, 8, canned and preserved fruits, and in cases on right in front are exhibits that must be of great interest, viz: The artistic display in bird work, and wax, and other figures, illustrating real life in Mexico; the first among the latter shows costumes of horsemen and women; next the method of making tortillas, (griddle cakes;) in same case, the method of gathering the pulque from the maguey; he draws it out and pours it in the sack which he carries on his back; still farther back, the water-carriers; above these the shoemaker, a porter, and Indian woman, with a load of charcoal upon her back for sale, &c. In next case, a court scene; a dancing girl showing one of the styles of wearing the rebozo, or long narrow shawl. Farther along, a fancy dress made of pith, of which you see specimens. These cost as high as $500. You now pass out of the Mexican Department toward the end of building and complete the examination of the Miscellaneous Exhibits as indicated by Guide, as much of this portion is of interest and should not be omitted.

MISCELLANEOUS.

Commencing at end of building with
G.G, 3, Riechle Bros., R. R. Scales.
G.G, 2, Marden's Standard Scales.
 Proceed towards front or east side.
H, 2, Becker Bros., Balances and Weights.
H, 3, John Matthews, Decorative Glass.
H, 3, Collier White Lead Co.
H.H and G, 3, Twisted Wire Box Strap.
H H, 2, L. Stephenson & Co., Balances and Scales.
H.H, 3, Merchant & Co., Tin Plates.
I, 2, Russell & Irwin, Builders' Hardware.

I, 3. St. Louis Lead and Oil Co.
I, 3. Penn. Wire Works.
I.I, 3, Geo. D. Wetherill & Co., Ready Mixed Paints.
I.I, 3, Indianapolis Terra Cotta Co.
I.I, 2, G. F. Atkins, California Novelties. Here see bark of California big tree, 18 inches thick. Illustration of big tree, 30 feet in diameter, with a carriage-way through it. It is 500 feet high, and 3,000 years old.
K.K, 2, C. H. Barton & Co., Wood Veneers, beautiful display; examine. Notice particularly snake wood and camphor wood.
L, 3, Le Paiges' Liquid Glue.
M, 3, Valentine & Co., Fine Coach Varnish.
M.M and M, 3, American Soap Stone Co.
N and M.M, 3, Hengley & Challenge, Roller Skates.
N, 3, Southern White Lead Co.
N, 3, Eastern Manufacturing Co.
N.N, 3, Thomas Christian, Ground Glue.
N.N, 2, Tenn. Lumber Co. See a poplar plank, 12 feet long, 3 inches thick, and 50 inches wide.
O, 2, The E. D. Albro Co. Veneers. One of the finest exhibits of the Exposition. Notice particularly burls (knots) of Persian and French walnut, birch and cherry, ebony, lignum-vitae, mahogany, and box-wood. The large, grayish, pulpy-looking mass you see is veneering cut, but not finished. The process of manufacturing veneering is as follows: The burl or knot is first steamed, then cut in very thin layers—as the one before you—then each layer is laid on a heated board background, after which hot rollers are passed over the veneer; it is then sand-papered and varnished. Their advertising card is printed on hollywood paper, the one hundred and sixtieth part of an inch thick.
O, 3, N. Y. Enamel Paint Co.
O, 2, Portevent & Farre, Lumber, &c.
O.O, 3, Gutta Percha Co., Paints.
P.P, 3, Union Paper Bag Co.
P, 3, George H. Wood & Co., Spanish Gloss.
Q. 3, Pyle's Pearline.
R and Q.Q, 3, Henry Woods, Son & Co., Manufacturers of Colors.
R, 2, Duryea's Mazena.
Going in direction of Music Hall, you come to
R and R.R, 5 and 6, Root & Peters, Mexican Goods. This is in some respects a novel and interesting exhibit, and should be examined carefully.
R and R.R, 7 and 8, S. Hemsheim, Cigars.
R and R.R, 9, J. Massman & Co., Fine Whiskies.
R, 9, John Wolf, Canes and Yankee Notions.
R and R.R, 9. Delpit, Tobacco and Snuff.
R and R.R, 11 and 12, Turkish Egyptian Goods.
R and R.R, 13, The Gross Pin Co.
R and R.R, 14, Fountain Ink Co.
R and R.R, 15, Caw's Ink.
R and R.R, 17 and 18, Chas. Scribner & Sons, Publications.
R.R, 20, Colby & Co., Adams' Historical Chart. Any person in any way interested in history, and parents especially, should examine this chart, for it

is a remarkable work, making history exceedingly interesting and at the same time very easily learned.

R.R, 21 and 22, E. Berg & Co., European Stitching and Stamping. Every lady should examine.

R and R.R, 22, The Columbian Type Writer.

Now pass on to

R.R, 25, Moseley & Co., Watch Makers' Tools.

R.R, 26, Keystone Watch Case Co. See exhibit.

R.R, 26 and 27, Waltham Watch Co. See fine watches and gems. The best watches here are $375. Diamonds are not used for watch jewels, for the finest watches are jewelled with rubies and sapphires. Cheaper watches have aqua marine and chrysolite. Notice in case splint diamonds and diamonds in rough. Turning about, return in next aisle to

R, 24 and 25, E. J. Hart & Co., Elastic Trusses.

R, 22 to 23, L. H. Thomas, Writing Inks.

R, 20 and 21, A. L. Redden, American Writing Machine. This is an excellent and interesting machine, a great saver of time and expense, and should be examined.

R, 20, MacKeller, Smiths & Jordan, Printers' Type, &c.

R, 14, C. J. Conley & Co., Rochester Rubber Stamp Works.

R, 13 and 14, Clagul, Schlicht & Field, Labor Saving Office Devices. Good. Business men should examine. You now examine the exhibits in the Gallery; it contains some of the finest and best exhibits of the Exposition. Proceed towards the south-east corner of building and take stairway to Gallery at that point.

GALLERY.

Entering the gallery, proceed westward to

T.T, 1 and 2, McIntosh Galvanic Faraday Battery Co.

T, 1 and 2, Poulson & Egan, Architectural Bronze; fine display.

T and S.S, 2, L. Schwartz, Marbleized Slates and Mantels; examine.

S.S and S, 1 and 2, Ky. Furniture Co., fine exhibit; examine.

S, 1 and 2, Sidney Squires & Co., Automatic Sofa Bed; examine.

R. R, 1 and 2, Gardner & Co., Perforated Veneer Chairs, &c.

R to Q.Q, 1 and 2, Heywood Bros. & Co., Chairs, Rattan and Reed Furniture; examine.

N.N, 1 and 2, Charles Tisch, Fine Furniture; examine.

N to K, 1 and 2, The Robert Mitchell Furniture Co. See carved and decorated furniture and stained glass. A complete dining and drawing-room, elegant exhibit; be sure to examine.

I and K, 1 and 2, Wakefield Rattan Co., Rattan and Reed Furniture, fine display; examine.

H, 1, Brunswick, Blake, Collender & Co., Billiard Furnishings; be sure and visit their elegantly fitted up billiard-room.

H.H and G.G, 1 and 2, Hertts Bros., Artistic Furniture. Their exhibit represents a room in an American gentleman's home. Notice the Sevre vases and brass clock on mantel; these alone are worth $1,000. The furnishing of the entire room is worth $10,000. As the room is lighted by electricity at night, it should be seen in its greatest beauty.

G. G, 2, R. Dinnel Bros., Fine Furniture.
G and F.F, 1 and 2, Phœnix Chair Co., Bent Goods.
F and F.F, 1 and 2, The Marks Adjustable Folding Chair Co., Adjustable Folding Chairs.
E to D. D, 1 and 2, H. R. Plimpton & Co., Sofa Beds; examine.
D. D to D, 1 and 2, Mathias Klein, Adjustable Chairs.
C and C.C, 12 and 13, Elkhart Carriage and Harness Manufacturing Co., Carriages, and Light and Heavy Harness.
C.C, 14, Excelsior Top Co., Leather and Rubber Carriage Tops.
C.C, 15, Dexter Spring Co., Dexter Queen Phaeton.
C.C, 16 to 19, J. M. Quinby & Co., Fine Carriages and Road Wagons, fine display.
C.C, 19 and 20, A. T. Demerest & Co., Fine Carriages.
C.C, 21, Henderson Buggy Bo., Carriages, Buggies, and Phaetons.
C.C, 23, Hiram W. Davis & Co., Buggies, Phaetons, and Carriages, fine display.
C.C, 25 to 27, Columbus Buggy Co., fine display, examine.
C.C, 29, The Renick, Curtis & Co., Road Carts.
C.C, 34 to 37, Milburn Manufacturing Co., carriages, fine exhibit; examine.
C.C, 37 to 41, James Cunningham, Son & Co., Hearses and Carriages; examine.
C.C, 41, R. P. Randall, Carriage and Harnesses, fine display.
C.C, 41 and 45, E. C. Fenner, Carriages; large and fine exhibit; see here a "Russian Drosky."
C.C, 46, Joseph Schwartz, Carriages and Wagons; fine display.
C.C, 47, Heald & Jones, The Graphite Lubricating Axle; examine.
C.C, 48, Robinson & Hitt, Omnibuses.
C.C, 48, A. F. Shuler, Automatic Jump-Seat; examine.
C.C, 49, William M. Farr, Sand, Mud, and Dust Bands for carriage axles; should be examined by all persons interested in carriages.
C and C.C, 49 to 51, Abbott Buggy Co., Carriages, and Perry's Patent Road Cart, which should be examined.
C.C, 52, The Steinbach Adjustable Baby Carriages; examine.
A and B, 52 and 53, Reichle Bros., Fine Carriages, Patent Two-Wheeler; examine.
A.A, 53 and 54, Hall Manufacturing Co., Patent Curry-Comb.
A.A, 54, Little & Larkin, Patent Automatic Jump-Seat Carriages.
A.A, 56, Sayers & Scoville, Fine Carriages and Hearses.
A.A, 57 and 58, Phineas Jones & Co., New Patent Split-Shaft Sulky.
A.A, 58, Berry Bros., Varnishes, celebrated Hard-Oil Finish.
A.A, 58, A. O. Abbott, Little Giant Hub Borers and Box Puller, with instructions as to setting carriage boxes.
A.A, 58, 59, and 60, Studebaker Bros., Manufacturing Co., Light Wagons and Carriages of all kinds; large display.
A.A, 60, G. Lengert & Son, Express Wagons.
A.A, 61, Richmond Transfer Co., Omnibuses.
A.A, 61 and 62, Edward Storm, Side-Bar Spring and Gears
B, 62, Crane Bros., Adjustable Bit and Harness Goods
B.B, 62, D. G. Miller, Hame-Fasteners; examine.
D, 62, Baker, Sloo & Co., Fine Carriages.
D.D and E, 62, Christina Carriage Factory, Carriages, Saddles, and Harnesses.
D.D and E, 62, A. Ortmayer & Son., Saddles and Harnesses.

E, 62, Monarch Rein Button Co., Rein Button Goods; examine.
E, 62, August Buermann, Horse Bits.
E, 62, F. Boardman, Patent Combination Collar and Fireman's Equipments; good thing; examine.
E.E, 62, Martin Weydig, Saddles and Harnesses.
E.E and F, 62, Peters and Calhon Co., Saddlery and Harness.
F, 62, The Daisy Sewing-Machine Co.
F and F.F, 62, Williams Manufacturing Co., Sewing-Machines.
H and H. 62, Singer Machine Co.; here you register your name and take your chance for a machine without cost.
K, 61, L. J. Duffy, Trunks, &c.
L and L.L, 62, Union Mfg. Co., Sewing-Machines and Wooden Ware.
M, 62, Globe Knitting Co., Family Knitting Machine.
M.M and M, 62, Schmit Bros. Trunk Co., Trunks, &c.
N and N.N, 62, Nashville Trunk Manufactury; examine.
O, 62, Suhr & Hauptmann, Curtain Chains.
P, 62, G. Koons, Refrigerator Co., fine display; examine.
P.P, 62, McBride & Co., Stone Filter, peculiar; examine.
Q.Q and R, 62, Fair Haven Slate Co; examine "the burning kettle" suspended from crane over fire-place of front mantel. This is a novel idea for grate ornament; also, fine display of paintings, &c. No one should fail to visit this exhibit.
S.S, 62, C. E. Anderson, Invalid Chair; examine.
S.S and T, 62, J. P. Tolman & Co., Cordage.
S.S and T, 62, M. Shutz, Novelties.
T, 62, M. Kaemper. The Moscowitz Model Waist Lining.
T.T, 62, H. J. Myers. La Moine Portable and Adjustable Dress Form.
T.T and U, 62, Thos. Potter, Sons & Co., Oil-Cloths.
T.T and U, 62, Weedsport Hoop Skirt Co.
U, 61 and 62, W. Friedrich, Horn Chairs.
U.U, 61, J. R. Palmenberg, Show Stands and Store Fixtures.
V, 60 and 59, Ready Cash Carrier.
V and V.V, 57 and 59, Standard Saloon Fixture Co., fine exhibit.
V, 55 and 56, The Buddington Dress-Cutting Machine.
V, 54 and 55, Cooper & McKee. Refrigerators, &c.
V, 53, Dape Bros. & Kugemann, Horn Furniture.
V, 53, Kursherd & Co., Furniture.
V, 49, Frederick Beck, Lincrusta Walton, a patent solid relief wall decoration, in imitation of terra-cotta, bronze, silver, gold, oak, &c., as solid as wood. This should receive careful examination.
V. 48, Union School Furniture Co.
V, 46 and 47, Edgefield and Nashville Mfg. Co., Builders, Furnishings, and House Furniture.
V, 46 and 47, Charles Gunold & Co., Invalid Bed, new patent and good; examine.
V, 45, Buffalo School Furniture Co. Notice New Paragon School Desk.
V, 43, J. H. Buford's Sons, Art and Advertising Cards.
V, 42, M. Thome, Hair Goods.
V, 41 and 40, Gillett & Gottschalk, Stamped Linens; examine.
V, 24, McCaw, Stephenson & Co., Stained Glass.

V, 23 and 24, W. C. Young, Stained Glass Institute.
V, 22 and 21, Olwatte Bros, Majolica, &c.
V, 19 and 20, Matthews & Willard Co. Brass Goods, beautiful; examine.
V and VV, 18 and 19, Saginaw Manufacturing Co., Shade Rollers and Wooden Ware; examine.
V, 16, J. Moore & Co., House Furnishings, &c.; good display.
V, 14, Thomas L. Leedon & Co., Carpets.
V, 13, M. & J. Ginoris, Artificial Flowers.
V, 9, Hubbard Hammock Co., Hammock Chair.
V, 9, C. J. Scholl, Self-acting Swing.
V, 7 and 8, James Wilson, Patent Blinds.
V, 2 and 4, Solon Palmer, Perfumes, &c.

Passing down the stairway at this place, proceed straight ahead, north, along "V. post," to first exit-way, from where you journey towards Horticultural Hall.

HORTICULTURAL HALL.

This building is 600 194 feet, and contains fruit exhibits from nearly every state and territory in the United States; from Russia, France, England, Mexico, and Central America; ferns and palm trees; plants from the Temperate and Tropical zones, and the largest collection of cacti and aloe family ever made. Upon entering the hall, turn to left and see the fine collection of California botanical exhibits, showing nearly every variety of tree or plant grown in both the temperate or tropical zones. Notice, particularly, the cinnamon tree, the acacia, the She oak of Australia, wonderfully adapted to barren regions; the caral tree, the same from which the Prodigal Son is supposed to have gathered the beans which he eat, the eucaliptus, or fever tree, which grows rapidly and absorbs malaria; the tea plant; the camphor tree. Pass farther along, and, on wall to left notice illustrations of the varieties (44) of Japanese oranges, from one half to ten inches in diameter. To the right of these, the sweet olives. Now, pass on to the fountain, which is surrounded by a large number of royal palms, which were brought from Mexico very beautiful; an immense cactus, twenty feet high, from Arizona. Just east of and near fountain, a fine date palm, showing stems that bore the dates; south and near fountain, one of the largest cocoanut palms in this country or Europe, thirty feet in height. West and beyond this, see group of bananas; the fruit grows from the center of main stalk.

Just beyond these, at end, see coffee tree; turning back to other side of building, enter the hot-house. On side wall see the orchids or air-plants from Central America, over 100 varieties they grow on trees, and have a very pretty flower with a peculiar odor. At farther end of hot-house in the south-west corner, you will see them lying on a shelf or table; turning around at south end, see pineapple and fruit, near which is the cotton plant, with blossoms and bolls. In center, the ginger plant, the root of which is used, known as ginger root; among the Jamaica plants, see the cinnamon, cloves, and breadfruit trees, the vanilla plant. See also Australian pines, and near, tree ferns, also the melon fruit bush, which bears a fruit resembling our cantaloupe—it will grow readily and is likely to come into common use. Passing from the hot-house to the Pomological Department, where the fruits of each state and territory are designated and can be examined, notice particularly the fruit display from Russia, England, and France in contrast with those of our own country. In the Florida exhibit, notice the shaddocks; grape fruit, a species of the orange, but not good to eat; the lime, from which lime juice is made, an antidote for scurvy. On Mexican table, notice a jar of pulque, the liquor of the maguey or century plant. When this pulque is first collected they use it for a drink, like our cider or beer—when it gets hard, it is made into alcohol, brandies, &c. On this table, also, see plantains, really large bananas, yams, or large variety of sweet potatoes, common potatoes—one species of which is supposed to resemble the wild species, as potatoes originated in the Andes. See immense yams on end of next table, and near them a cluster of cocoanuts. In this part of hall, in south-western corner, see the Mexican plants, among which the acacia, the agave, the sappho-dilla, which produces a small delicious fruit, the alligator pear. Now passing to front, or north end, on west side, you come to the very large collection of cacti, among which notice one having a long, grayish, hairy growth surrounding the plant called the "old-man-cactus." Further along, a club-like cactus, called the organ cactus. Farther along toward the door, see the cochineal cactus and the insects from which the cochineal is obtained. Near the end of this table, see snake cactus, valued at $300. It is a peculiar and very rare species. Passing out of the Hall, turn to your left, and go to a group of maguey, or century plants, where you can see how the Mexicans form the basin that collects the pulque in first or second plant and covered. After examining these, return and go to the Art Gallery.

ART GALLERY.

This Art Hall is a spacious fire-proof structure, 250 feet long and 100 feet deep, furnishing 20,000 square feet of hanging space; splendidly lighted during the day by sky-lights, and during the evening by 2,000 Edison incandescent electric lights. The building is divided into four large halls, three on the front and a fourth running parallel and occupying one half the building, 50 x 250 feet. Entering through the broad vestibule, we pass the Superintendent's office on the right and the Committee-room on the left, and enter the central hall, 50 feet square, filled with sculpture, consisting of marbles, bronzes, terra-cottas, rilievos, and plaster casts which stand forth prominently against the dark brown walls. The works shown are by French, Belgian, Italian, English, and American artists. Among those that will attract the attention of visitors are:

"THE PIGEONS OF ST. MARK'S."
By Brunin.

L'IMPRUDENT AND L'AMOUR MALADROIT.
By Samain.

TRIBOULET.
By Willem.

CARLIST.
By Bruneau.

Mr. A. Bruce Joy, of London, shows a beautiful work entitled "The First Flight," also several busts of merit, among which those of "Gladstone" and "Mary Anderson" should be noted, as should also the strong head in bronze of "Bryant," by Hartley, of New York, and of "Beethoven," by Valentine,

ART GALLERY --- 300 X 100 FEET.

HORTICULTURAL HALL, 600X100 FEET.

www.ingramcontent.com/pod-product-compliance
Lightning Source LLC
Chambersburg PA
CBHW031120160426
43192CB00008B/1058